COOKING
FROM SCRATCH
FOR TEENS

COOKING FROM SCRATCH
FOR TEENS

MAKE YOUR OWN HEALTHY & DELICIOUS FOOD

LISA BURNS
creator of This Pilgrim Life

PAGE STREET
PUBLISHING CO.

PAGE STREET
PUBLISHING CO.

First published in 2023 by

Page Street Publishing Co.

27 Congress Street, Suite 1511

Salem, MA 01970

www.pagestreetpublishing.com

Distributed by Macmillan, sales in Canada by The Canadian Manda Group.

27   26   25   24   23   1   2   3   4   5

ISBN-13: 978-1-64567-914-1

ISBN-10: 1-64567-914-4

Library of Congress Control Number: 2022949688

Cover and book design by Laura Benton and Emma Hardy for Page Street Publishing Co.
Photography by Ken Goodman

Printed and bound in the United States of America

DEDICATION

For anyone starting on their culinary journey.
May you discover how rewarding and delicious it can be.

CONTENTS

Introduction 11

AWESOME MAIN DISHES IN ONE PAN 21

Easy Cheesy Enchiladas 23

Roasted Sausage with Perfectly Crisp Potatoes & Veg 24

Creamy Chicken & Broccoli Soup 27

Homemade Meatball Sub Sandwiches 28

Your First Amazing Chicken Curry 31

Sweet & Tangy Grilled Chicken Kabobs 32

Chicken Pot Pie Made Easy 35

Easy Pork Fried Rice 36

Tater Tot Supreme 39

Fancy Lasagna with No Layering 40

THESE ARE CLASSICS FOR A REASON 43

The Best Steak Ever 45

Killer Fettuccine Alfredo 46

Share-the-Love Cozy Chicken Noodle Soup 49

Super Easy Pizza with Endless Possibilities 50

Now & Later Spaghetti Bake 53

Epic Meat Lovers' Chili 54

Homestyle Baked Mac 'n' Cheese 57

Sliders with an Upgrade 58

Amazing Homemade Bread in 1 Hour
(French, Sub Rolls & Cinnamon Raisin Buns) 61

Perfect Late-Night Omelet 66

EAT YOUR VEGGIES   69

Mexican Street Corn Made Easy   71
Awesome Caesar Salad Wraps   72
Hiker's Salad with Creamy Citrus Poppyseed Dressing   75
Sweet & Savory Veggie Soup   76
Energy-Boosting Green Smoothie   79
Unbelievably Delicious Veg Tart   80
Pasta & Veggie Soup to Fill You Up   83
Perfect Roasted Vegetables   84

HUNGRY AGAIN? SNACKS THAT SATISFY   87

Better-for-You Instant Ramen   89
Overloaded Potato Wedges   90
Next-Level Grilled Cheese Sandwiches   93
Chocolate Chip Muffins with a Twist   94
Everyone's Favorite Tuna Salad   97
Ridiculously Good Ham Sliders   98
Awesome Black Bean Taquitos   101
Take-Anywhere Energy Bites   102

I'LL TAKE MY BREAKFAST TO GO   105

Best Ever Breakfast Sandwiches   107
Stuffed French Toast   108
Peanut Butter & Chocolate Protein Smoothie   111
Better-than-Boxed Toaster Pastries   112
Healthy Egg Bites   115
Super Easy Grab-&-Go Overnight Oatmeal   116
Killer Breakfast Burritos   119
Homemade Mocha Frappuccino   120

EPIC FOOD FOR PARTIES & GATHERINGS 123

Sweet & Salty White Chocolate Bark	125
Totally Loaded Nachos	126
Crazy Delicious Hot Dog Bar	129
Homemade Potato Chip Dip	130
The Best Party Popcorn	133
Firepit Chicken Fajitas	134
Decadent Hot Chocolate with Spruced Up Marshmallows	137
Comeback Snack Mix	138

THIS CALLS FOR SOMETHING SPECIAL 141

Legendary Double Cookie Ice Cream Cake	143
Easiest Apple Pie & Homemade Whipped Cream	144
Ooey-Gooey S'mores Cookies	147
Last-Minute Confetti Cookie Cake	148
Impressive Chocolate Pudding Pie	151
Amazing Mini Pound Cakes	152
Epic PB Cup Brownies	155
Super Fun Banana Split Milkshakes	156

Acknowledgments	159
About the Author	161
Index	162

INTRODUCTION

Knowing how to cook is incredibly empowering. Being able to turn basic ingredients into a finished dish is its own kind of superpower.

As awesome as that feeling of empowerment is, it's important to expect it to feel challenging at times too. Don't get discouraged if you have to read the recipe a few times or if a dish doesn't come out perfectly on the first (or second) attempt. That's completely normal! And it is normal for beginner and experienced cooks alike.

My teenage son, Jack, loves cooking and creating new dishes in the kitchen. He helped me during the developing, testing and photographing of many of these recipes. Even with all this experience, he is still eager to keep learning and building his skills because there is always more to learn in the kitchen.

Thankfully, one of the best things about cooking is that you can learn in spits and spurts, at your own pace, with your own priorities. Is it more important to you to learn first how to bake a loaf of bread? Make a quick dinner? Or bake a tasty treat to share with friends? It's your choice.

If you haven't done much cooking before now, you may have an idea that cooking has to look like what you've seen on your phone or TV—matching prep bowls, a dozen dishes and complicated recipes. Trust me when I say that when you are in your own kitchen, not cooking for an audience, the process can be greatly simplified.

So, relax a bit. Shake off any expectations (yours or your parents') that just because you're holding this cookbook that you're destined to be the next master chef, or at the least, in charge of making all your meals from now on.

The point of this cookbook, of learning to cook in general, is simply to equip you with skills and options for a better life.

"Better how?" you may ask. Preparing your own food gives you control over your ingredients and the skill to turn a small bag of groceries into a delicious meal. Cooking can be a stress reliever, a creative outlet, a way to save money and an important part of a healthy lifestyle.

What's more, knowing how to cook opens all kinds of opportunities to bring people together. There's no need to only rely on cheap pizzas for parties (no need to cut that option out completely either), when you can quickly whip up a huge batch of nachos or impress your friends with an awesome hot dog bar and surprise them with ingenious toppings.

Or maybe you're thinking of cooking a special dinner for a date—winning them over with an incredible steak or a bowl of authentic Italian pasta. Just be sure to practice once or twice first so you don't lose face with a flopped meal!

Learning to cook is worth the time and effort. I want this empowerment for you! I hope this cookbook will be a gateway into a life of feeling confident in the kitchen and enjoying countless tasty meals in the days ahead.

Lisa Burns

TOP TEN TIPS FOR LEARNING TO COOK (AND USING THIS COOKBOOK)

The recipes in this cookbook were selected and crafted with you in mind. Whether you are satisfying an afternoon craving, prepping on-the-go breakfasts for the week ahead, making a fun dish for a party or something else—these recipes are simple and accessible for a cook at any level.

Before you jump into the book (or perhaps more realistically, whenever you decided to visit the introduction), I have ten basic tips for success in the kitchen. These tips are universal. There's no growing out of them—only more fully experiencing their practical usefulness.

1. COOKING GETS EASIER . . . AND FOOD WILL TASTE BETTER.

One of the most important things to remember anytime you are learning something new, whether in the kitchen or on the field or in the classroom, is that it will get easier. The job may feel awkward at first, and it may take longer than you'd like, but keep at it.

Eventually you'll learn where everything is kept without having to ask, your knife skills will improve, recipes won't seem like reading a foreign language and cooking tasty meals will take less time.

In addition to all that, you'll also find that with consistent practice and regular effort, your food will turn out better. With experience, you'll be able to recognize what ingredients should look like at different points, be able to taste and adjust as you go and know how to finish dishes just right.

Don't give up and definitely don't think it's only you having a hard time. A learning curve is real no matter what you're learning. You just have to give yourself enough chances to make the transition from learning to knowing.

Remember, a new skill or recipe is only completely new once. Every time you work in the kitchen, you are making it better for the next time.

2. USE FEWER, BETTER TOOLS.

You don't need the most expensive kitchen equipment or a specific tool for every ingredient.

A quality knife, regularly sharpened, is hands-down the most important tool to have in your kitchen. Not only is a dull knife more dangerous (requiring more force and more prone to slipping), using a dull knife is annoying. The same goes for using a knife that is too small for the job.

Thankfully, a quality knife does not need to break the bank. My favorite knives that I use daily are Victorinox. They're affordable, reliable, sharpen well and hold an edge.

Besides a chef's knife, having a few other quality kitchen tools can be very helpful. Again, focus on quality over quantity—fewer tools that can do a variety of jobs. The tools I have found to make the biggest difference are a good peeler, one-piece silicon spatulas, a pair of stainless steel tongs, wooden spoons, a stainless steel whisk and a box grater (shredding your own cheese is very helpful when making sauces so the cheese melts properly).

3. READ THE DIRECTIONS FIRST. TWICE.

Don't skip this! Getting halfway through a recipe and suddenly realizing you are missing a crucial ingredient, or don't have the time needed to complete the recipe is the worst.

Always read through the recipe from start to finish. Double-check you have everything you need. This is also a great time to gather your bowls, pans and so on.

4. START STRONG.

It is often tempting to jump right in when beginning a recipe and to complete the steps as you go, but in many recipes, you're better off prepping your ingredients before getting started. Often a recipe progresses rather quickly once begun. You won't have time to prep ingredients between steps (for example, your butter could burn while you're dicing onions).

Although it may seem counterintuitive, spending 10 minutes at the beginning to gather and prepare ingredients will save you time when you are moving through the recipe. Being prepared will also help you avoid feeling rushed or behind, meaning you're less likely to make avoidable mistakes.

Start on the right foot and find that the process is more enjoyable.

5. QUALITY INGREDIENTS MATTER.

Do you want to know one of the fastest ways to make your dishes taste better? Start with good ingredients! This doesn't mean selecting the most expensive items on the shelf, but it does mean reading labels and paying attention to freshness.

Generally, starting with whole ingredients gives you more control over the end results. I do a majority of our cooking "from scratch"—preparing my own sauces, spice blends and so on.

This cookbook finds a balance between from-scratch cooking and convenience. Some things I show you how to make yourself (like pudding for the homemade pie in the dessert chapter), but many others call for ready-to-go sauces and dressings.

Find quality ingredients by choosing ones with shorter ingredient lists, preferably ones in which you can recognize the names of most of the components. Both fresh and frozen vegetables are great options, though you may prefer one over the other for different recipes.

6. GIVE YOURSELF A GOOD FOUNDATION FIRST.

One of the greatest things about learning to cook, and especially learning to cook from scratch, is that you can make recipes your own. You can play with flavors and ingredients and try new variations.

However, a good rule of thumb is to not make any significant changes the first time you make a recipe. Following the recipe as it is written will give you an understanding of how the dish is put together.

As you explore cooking, you will figure out what swaps work and which ones do not. If you are wanting to make a change to vegetables, for instance, try to select a substitute vegetable that is similar to the one you are omitting so the cooking time remains the same— root vegetables can usually be used interchangeably, but you wouldn't want to cook a zucchini in the same way you would a potato or carrot.

Give yourself a solid foundation of using a variety of recipes, techniques and cooking methods, and then don't be afraid to have fun in the kitchen and try new things!

7. COOK ONCE, EAT MANY TIMES.

Whether you like to cook or not, this tip is a game changer—a time saver, a money saver, a nutrition saver. Cooking more than you need for the next meal is working smarter, not harder.

Your life is busy and you probably don't want to spend more time than you need to in the kitchen. I get it! Batch cooking is a great way to make the most of small pockets of time when you have the opportunity to prep food.

Trade an hour in the kitchen for breakfasts all week, make enough dinner so that you can freeze the leftovers for another night or prepare snacks that will fill you up better than a bag of chips.

Keep your busy schedule and vibrant social life, knowing that you have food you've already prepped waiting for you.

Your future self will thank you.

If you find that you have leftovers regularly and would like a convenient way to freeze them in perfect portions, consider investing in silicon freezer trays. My favorites are from Souper Cubes®, and I have them in all different sizes. I love using them to freeze leftover Now & Later Spaghetti Bake (page 53), extra Epic Meat Lovers' Chili (page 54) and even extra Energy-Boosting Green Smoothie (page 79).

8. DON'T UNDERESTIMATE THE POWER OF A GOOD SAUTÉ.

Sautéing and roasting (next tip) are simultaneously two of the simplest and most effective ways to develop flavor in food. Using high heat when cooking certain foods produces the Maillard reaction. I'll spare you the scientific explanation. In short, the combination of heat, food and time results in browning and richer flavor (than the same food cooked at a lower heat).

Simple as it is, there are a few guidelines to follow to achieve a good sauté:

- Heat your pan before adding food. You can test a pan's readiness by hovering your hand over the pan to feel the radiating heat, or add oil, butter or a couple drops of water and wait for it to foam/sizzle.

- Arrange your food in a flat layer on the pan. Contact with the pan is essential for a good sauté, so it's important not to overcrowd the food. Use a large enough pan for the recipe, or sauté in batches if necessary.

- Resist the urge to stir/flip too soon/often. Food cooked with high heat will develop a "crust" when it has achieved a good sear. For example, if you put a chicken breast in a hot pan and try to move it immediately, it will stick and tear. But if you wait until the chicken is browned, it will easily release from the pan. This is also important for vegetables. After adding the vegetables and giving them a stir to coat them with the oil, butter and/or seasonings, leave them alone in the pan for several minutes to give them time to soften and brown.

My absolute favorite pans for sautéing are cast-iron (specifically Lodge brand). While cast-iron pans may have a reputation for being fussy or difficult, they're actually quite easy to use once you get the hang of them. Cast-iron pans heat evenly and hold heat well, making them a perfect conduit for the Maillard reaction. If you want to learn more about cooking with cast-iron, you can find resources and tips on my website, thispilgrimlife.com/cast-iron.

9. CRANK UP THE HEAT AND CRANK UP THE FLAVOR (ROASTING IS MORE THAN A GOOD BURN).

Like sautéing, roasting food on a baking sheet in a very hot oven creates an environment for food to develop rich, deep flavors. Vegetables in particular are so tasty when roasted! If you think you don't like a vegetable, don't rule it out completely before trying it roasted (see the recipe for Perfect Roasted Vegetables on page 84).

The guidelines for roasting are similar to those for sautéing, with the exception of preheating your pan. Instead, you preheat your oven. The other two guidelines apply—arrange the food in a flat layer and do not stir too often.

A large rimmed baking sheet that has a little weight to it is ideal for roasting. My favorite baking sheets are the half-sheet and three-quarter sheet corrugated baking sheets from William-Sonoma. They are 18 x 13 x 1 inch (46 x 33 x 2.5 cm) and 21 x 15 x 1 inch (53 x 38 x 2.5 cm), respectively. Like a good skillet, a quality baking sheet can be used for countless recipes and foods.

10. KNOW YOUR WHY.

We've arrived at the last tip, saved purposefully for the end. Why does all this matter? Why spend time in the kitchen? Why use this cookbook?

You will discover your own motivations as you cook, enjoy your meals and share them with others. You will likely even find that your "why" will change and shift in different seasons of your life.

Eating out can get expensive really quickly, even just regularly purchasing special coffee drinks and juices. Making your own homemade versions of some of your favorite menu items will mean more money in the bank and more money for whatever else matters to you more than fast food or a fancy latte.

Perhaps you find that you enjoy the creativity that cooking and baking brings you—maybe you learn to love food photography or make super fun food videos to share.

Or maybe, like my oldest son, you're just happy eating especially tasty food. You don't want to settle for bland or boring, so you learn to cook and make dishes that SING WITH FLAVOR (it's a thing—just ask Jack).

Whatever the reason, I hope you will discover how fun food and cooking can be, and I hope you will discover the power and satisfaction that even the humblest food can hold!

Dear reader, the cooking journey ahead of you is exciting, diverse and limitless.

Enjoy it! Share it! Savor it!

AWESOME MAIN DISHES IN ONE PAN

One-pan dinners are hugely popular with good reason—they're convenient, often quick-cooking and in the case of many of the recipes in this chapter, they often include shortcuts that speed up the process of making dinner even more. Plus, you'll save yourself a lot of dishwashing since there's only one pan. If you're looking for a delicious dinner idea to make for your family, this chapter is just what you need. Or, maybe you're looking to make a tasty meal and have some left over for later in the week. Either way, I've got you covered.

The one-pan main recipes in this chapter are anything but boring. Convenience and shortcuts do not have to be synonymous with bland flavors or typical dishes! All the components of these dishes may be all together (making preparation so easy), but what you end up with are finished dishes that still look complex and colorful.

Curry, lasagna, enchiladas, pot pie and more using only one piece of kitchen equipment— no need to sacrifice any "wow" factor here!

My go-to equipment for one-pan meals that make plenty to go around are a 12-inch (30-cm) cast-iron skillet, a large roasting pan and a 7-quart (6.7-L) Dutch oven or soup pot. Each of these are incredibly versatile and useful to have on hand. If you have each of these, the variety of meals you can make in them is unlimited.

EASY CHEESY ENCHILADAS

SERVINGS: 6

Create a colorful and flavorful fiesta on your plate with these amazing one-pan enchiladas! You're going to love how simple it is to make this twist on a Mexican classic. The deep flavor of the sauce and the heartiness of the beef pair perfectly with your favorite toppings like sour cream, guacamole and cheese! Finishing this dish with fresh pico de gallo (similar to salsa) that you whipped up yourself is sure to get you mad props too.

This dish is a prime example of how quality ingredients elevate a recipe's final tastiness. The fresher your produce and the higher the quality of your protein, the better the final results. Mexican and Tex-Mex food especially highlight this principle. Try the fresh Pico de Gallo on Totally Loaded Nachos (page 126) or Awesome Black Bean Taquitos (page 101) next!

Preheat the oven to 350°F (177°C).

In a large skillet (about 10 to 12 inches [25 to 30 cm]), combine the ground beef, diced green pepper and diced onion. Stir to incorporate, and then add the seasonings—cumin, oregano, chili powder, garlic powder and kosher salt—and stir again. Cook the ground beef mixture over medium heat until the meat is no longer pink and the vegetables are tender. This should take 5 to 10 minutes. Once the meat is almost completely browned, you can use your spoon or spatula to break up the meat until it is finely crumbled. Drain any excess grease.

Stir in the enchilada sauce, broken-up pieces of corn tortillas and 1 cup (113 g) of the cheese. Top the mixture with the remaining cup (113 g) of cheese, spreading it evenly across the top of the mixture.

Transfer the enchilada skillet to the oven and bake for 15 minutes.

While the enchilada skillet bakes, make the pico de gallo. Combine the diced tomatoes, minced jalapeño, minced onion, cilantro leaves, lime juice and kosher salt in a bowl and stir well to incorporate all the components and flavors. Chill in the fridge until you serve the enchilada skillet.

When the timer goes off, carefully remove the hot skillet from the oven. Let it stand 5 minutes before serving. Top the enchilada bake with pico de gallo or other suggested topping ideas. Serve with tortilla chips on the side.

TEEN CHEF TIP: Be careful when you are slicing the jalapeño because the oils on the inside can make your skin burn if you touch your face after touching the jalapeño. Some cooks prefer to wear gloves for this reason. You can determine the heat in your pico de gallo by choosing to keep in the jalapeño seeds or to discard them. The more seeds you keep, the higher the heat.

1 lb (454 g) ground beef

1 green pepper, diced

½ cup (80 g) diced yellow onion

1 tsp ground cumin

1 tsp dried oregano

1 tsp chili powder

1 tsp garlic powder

½ tsp kosher salt

2½ cups (600 ml) jarred or canned enchilada sauce (I really like Hatch Red Enchilada Sauce®)

8 (6-inch [15-cm]) corn tortillas, roughly torn into 2-inch (5-cm) pieces

2 cups (226 g) shredded Mexican blend cheese

PICO DE GALLO

2 cups (360 g) diced tomatoes

1 medium jalapeño, minced (see Teen Chef Tip)

½ cup (80 g) minced yellow onion

2 tbsp (2 g) fresh cilantro leaves

1 tbsp (15 ml) lime juice

½ tsp kosher salt

OPTIONAL ADDITIONAL TOPPINGS

Sour cream

Store-bought guacamole

Corn salsa

Sliced ripe avocado

Cilantro

Tortilla chips

ROASTED SAUSAGE WITH PERFECTLY CRISP POTATOES & VEG

SERVINGS: 4–5

1 lb (454 g) sweet Italian sausage links, sliced into 1-inch (2.5-cm) pieces

1 medium yellow onion, cut in half, then quartered

2 cups (256 g) sliced carrots, about 4–5 carrots

3 cups (450 g) quartered red potatoes, about 6-8 potatoes

1 cup (85 g) halved brussels sprouts

DRESSING
¼ cup (60 ml) olive oil

2 tbsp (30 ml) red wine vinegar

2 tbsp (30 ml) honey

1 tsp kosher salt

1 tsp red chili flakes

1 tsp granulated garlic

You will definitely want to mark this recipe for nights when you need an extra easy recipe that doesn't require any babysitting while it cooks. Sweet Italian sausage and hearty root vegetables get tossed together in a simple tangy dressing, before roasting in the oven for an hour, giving you the perfect opportunity to go outside to practice for an upcoming game, catch an episode of a favorite show or even sneak in a little homework (just be sure to set an alarm to give the mixture a quick stir halfway through).

Another option is to prep the mixture earlier in the day, or the night before, and leave it in the fridge until you are ready to roast everything on a sheet pan. Don't be fooled by this recipe's simplicity though—all that time it's roasting and you're doing other things, the mixture is building extreme flavor on its own in the oven. This meal pairs really well with a loaf of 1-hour French bread (page 61) and warm applesauce with cinnamon.

Preheat oven to 400°F (204°C).

Combine the prepared sausages, yellow onion, sliced carrots, red potatoes and brussels sprouts in a large bowl.

To make the dressing, stir together the olive oil, red wine vinegar, honey, kosher salt, red chili flakes and granulated garlic in a liquid measuring cup, and then pour the dressing over the sausages and vegetables. Toss the mixture well so the dressing coats all the pieces.

Transfer the mixture to a large, low-rimmed baking sheet. Spread everything into as flat of a layer as possible so the sausages and vegetables are all touching the pan. Alternately, if your baking sheet is on the smaller size, you can divide the mixture up between two baking sheets to roast side by side. Having too much on the pan, or using a pan with tall sides, will result in the mixture not properly caramelizing.

Bake the sausages and vegetables in the preheated oven for 1 hour, stirring everything after 30 minutes, making sure to return everything to a flat layer on the pan.

TEEN CHEF TIP: When roasting vegetables for an extended time, like in this recipe, the pieces should be larger than what you would do for a soup or sauté. Chunkier 1-inch (2.5-cm) pieces will hold up longer under the high heat, giving the vegetables time to both soften and develop flavor. Similarly, when roasting several different types of vegetables and meat together on a sheet pan, cutting everything the same general size helps to ensure a consistent cooking time for the entire tray.

CREAMY CHICKEN & BROCCOLI SOUP

Creamy broccoli soup is a popular soup to order out, but restaurant soup is often loaded with excess sodium, potentially leading to very not-fun results like puffiness and water retention. No thanks. Skip the sodium spike and make this delicious chicken and broccoli soup at home! Pick up pre-chopped broccoli and a pack of chicken breasts and you'll be amazed with how easy this soup is to make.

This recipe also calls for wild rice, which is one of my favorite ingredients to include in a soup because it imparts such a nice nutty flavor to the broth. Everything all cooks together, resulting in a hearty soup that is both cozy and filling. Adding heavy cream and Parmesan cheese at the end is a simple way to take a soup from good to great!

2 tbsp (30 ml) olive oil

1 cup (160 g) minced yellow onion

1 cup (110 g) finely diced carrot, about 4-5 carrots

1½ tsp (9 g) kosher salt, divided

2 boneless, skinless chicken breasts

½ tsp fresh ground pepper

3 cups (273 g) chopped broccoli florets

⅓ cup (66 g) wild rice

⅓ cup (66 g) brown rice

4 cups (960 ml) chicken stock

2 cups (480 ml) water

½ cup (120 ml) heavy cream

½ cup (50 g) shredded Parmesan cheese, plus more for serving if needed

Place a large soup pot on the stove over medium heat. Once the pan feels warm when you hold your hand just above the bottom, add the olive oil, minced onion and diced carrot. Season the vegetables with ½ teaspoon of kosher salt, stir and then let the vegetables sauté and begin to soften for about 5 minutes.

Pat the chicken breasts dry (use a clean paper towel and then immediately discard), and then season both sides with 1 teaspoon of kosher salt and the fresh ground pepper. Once the vegetables have sautéed for roughly 5 minutes, push them to the sides of the pot and add the chicken breasts to the center of the pot. Brown the chicken for 3 to 4 minutes on the first side, and then flip the chicken over to brown the other side for 3 to 4 minutes more.

After the chicken has browned on both sides, add the broccoli, the wild rice and brown rice, chicken stock and water.

Bring the soup to a low simmer, cover and cook for 20 minutes, until the chicken is cooked through (the temperature measures 170°F [77°C] with a digital thermometer inserted in the thickest part).

Remove the chicken from the soup pot, use two forks to shred the meat, and then return it to the soup. Stir in the cream and Parmesan cheese.

Serve immediately, topping with additional Parmesan cheese if desired.

TEEN CHEF TIP: Brown rice and wild rice work well together in this soup because they have similar cook times, which is similar to whole chicken breasts. If you wanted to substitute a different rice, like long grain white rice, you would need to reduce the overall cook time by half. To shorten the cooking time for the chicken, dice it into 1-inch (2.5-cm) pieces before sautéing.

HOMEMADE MEATBALL SUB SANDWICHES

2 cups (480 g) marinara sauce

4 cups (1.7 kg) frozen meatballs

½ cup (80 g) diced yellow onion

½ cup (58 g) diced green pepper

1 tsp dried basil

6 (6-inch [15-cm]) sub rolls

3 cups (336 g) shredded mozzarella cheese

No need to go out to a sandwich shop for meatball subs when they're this easy to make at home! Pro tip: Keep marinara sauce in the pantry, and meatballs and mozzarella in the freezer and you'll be able to make a batch of subs whenever the craving hits. Did you know you can also freeze bread?! Double-bag sub rolls and toss them in the freezer! Now you have the basics for an easy Italian sub sandwich any time—midnight subs, anyone?

If you're making a pan of these for dinner and have a little extra time, you can elevate this recipe and wow your family by making your own sub rolls in just an hour (page 61). Serve these meatball subs with a bagged salad or some chips for a simple, crowd-pleasing dinner.

Heat the marinara sauce and meatballs together in a medium bowl in the microwave, or a pot on the stove, until the mixture is hot to the touch. Stir in the diced onion, green pepper and basil.

Lay the sub rolls open on a baking sheet. Divide the sauce and meatball mixture between the subs, spreading it on one side of the rolls. Top the sauce and meatball mixture with the shredded cheese, this time covering both sides of the open rolls.

Place the sandwiches in the oven using the broil function to melt the cheese and toast the edges of the sandwiches.

TEEN CHEF TIP: The broil function on the oven is very handy for toasting the tops of food, melting cheese on finished dishes, etc. However, it's also very easy to accidentally burn food if it's forgotten for even just a few minutes. When you're using the broil function, always set a timer and stay nearby so you're ready to pull your food out at just the right time.

YOUR FIRST AMAZING CHICKEN CURRY

The next time you want to enjoy a meal that is anything but boring and basic, you're going to want to make this easy curry! Don't blame me if you find it hard to resist eating it straight from the pan after you taste the rich, flavorful gravy-like sauce. If you can resist, definitely serve this curry over rice, maybe with naan bread on the side.

If you've never had curry, this recipe offers an easy way to give it a try and enjoy curry on any night at home. Because you use a premade curry sauce, you can choose how spicy or mild you would like the finished dish. Pick a mild sauce for a cozy bowl of curry, or select a hotter sauce if you prefer more of a kick. If you're a fan of living dangerously and want even more heat, you can double the chili powder or top your bowl of curry with a favorite hot sauce!

1 tsp turmeric

½ tsp ground cumin

½ tsp ground ginger

½ tsp kosher salt

½ tsp chili powder

2 tbsp (28 g) ghee

2 boneless, skinless chicken breasts

½ cup (80 g) minced yellow onion

1 tbsp (9 g) minced garlic

1 (12.5-oz [340-g]) jar curry sauce (my favorite brands are Maya Kaimal® and Brooklyn Delhi®)

1 (13.5-oz [399-ml]) can coconut milk

1 cup (134 g) frozen peas, thawed

2 (8-oz [224-g] packages microwave rice) or 1 (20-oz [560-g]) package frozen rice

OPTIONAL TOPPINGS

Fresh cilantro

Dollop of Greek yogurt

Minced red onion

Chopped lightly salted peanuts

Hot sauce

Naan bread

Combine the turmeric, cumin, ginger, kosher salt and chili powder in a small dish. Heat the ghee in a skillet over medium heat. Cut the chicken into 1-inch (2.5-cm) pieces, and then season them with the spice mixture, tossing the chicken so the pieces are evenly coated. Add the cubed chicken to the hot pan and brown for about 6 minutes, stirring after 3 minutes to brown the other sides of the pieces.

Push the chicken to the sides in the pan. Add the minced onion and garlic to the center of the pan and sauté for about 5 minutes, just until the onion is beginning to soften and the garlic is fragrant. After 5 minutes, stir to combine the chicken, onion and garlic.

Pour in the curry sauce and the coconut milk. Stir in the peas and mix until everything is well incorporated.

Bring the curry mixture to a low simmer and cook for 15 minutes.

Follow the package instructions to heat your rice. Serve the curry over the rice or with naan bread. Add extra toppings if desired.

TEEN CHEF TIP: There are several options for selecting a rice that will keep this recipe super easy. Microwave rice is available in different varieties, like a hearty brown rice or a fluffy white rice. You can also find ready-to-heat rice in the freezer section of many grocery stores. A final option is to make a large batch of rice another day and freeze it in smaller portions to enjoy with dishes like this curry. Freeze the rice flat in a freezer-safe bag. To reheat, transfer the frozen rice to a heat-safe bowl, add a couple tablespoons of water, and cover with a lightly damp paper towel. Heat in the microwave for 2 to 3 minutes, or until hot. To reheat on the stove, transfer the frozen rice to a small pot with a couple tablespoons of water. Heat on low until hot.

SWEET & TANGY GRILLED CHICKEN KABOBS

Fire up the grill for these delicious marinated chicken and vegetable kabobs! Grilling is a surefire way to rocket your food's flavor way up. Those slightly blackened edges are the true taste of summer. What's even better, kabobs are a simple, beginner-friendly way to learn how to use a grill! With all the ingredients cut into bite-sized pieces, they fit together conveniently on skewers, making them easy to transport and quick to cook. Check the forecast, call your friends up and put this recipe on the menu when the weather looks nice.

Cut the chicken breasts into approximately 2-inch (5-cm) pieces. Mix together the marinade ingredients—¼ cup (60 ml) olive oil, soy sauce, honey, ginger and garlic—in a liquid measuring cup or small bowl. Add the cubed chicken to a zipper bag, shallow bowl or baking dish. Pour in the marinade and mix well. Seal the bag or cover the bowl/dish. Refrigerate for at least 4 hours, up to 24 hours.

When you are ready to assemble the kabobs, prepare the crookneck yellow squash and zucchini by cutting them into 1-inch (2.5-cm) slices, followed by tossing the pieces into a medium-sized mixing bowl with the remaining olive oil, salt and pepper. Remove the chicken from the refrigerator and discard any excess marinade.

Assemble the kabobs by skewering the chicken and vegetables in an alternating pattern. Place the assembled kabobs in a large baking dish or baking sheet until you are ready to transfer them to the grill.

Clean the grill if needed and then turn it on to medium heat. Once the grill is hot, carefully place on the kabobs using a pair of long grilling tongs. Let the kabobs cook for about 8 minutes before flipping them to cook on the other side. You want to wait to flip the kabobs until the meat has a good sear to prevent it from sticking or tearing.

Use a pair of grilling tongs to flip the kabobs (use a second pair to help if the kabobs want to spin when you flip them). Cook for another 7 to 8 minutes, until the chicken is cooked through (reads 165°F [74°C] inside with an instant read meat thermometer) and the vegetables are tender.

Remove the kabobs from the grill to a large serving plate or baking sheet and loosely cover them with foil until you are ready to eat.

SERVINGS: 4–5

3 boneless, skinless chicken breasts

¼ cup + 2 tbsp (90 ml) olive oil, divided

2 tbsp (30 ml) soy sauce

2 tbsp (30 ml) honey

1 tbsp (14 g) fresh ginger, minced

1 tbsp (9 g) fresh garlic, minced

2 crookneck yellow squash

2 zucchini

½ tsp kosher salt

½ tsp pepper

8–10 metal skewers

TEEN CHEF TIP
THREE TIPS FOR BETTER GRILLING

1. Preheat the grill 10 to 15 minutes before you start cooking. This will also make it easier to clean off any food stuck on the grill grates after the grill is hot. Use a grill brush to scrape off bits of food before cooking anything new.

2. Keep space between the food you are cooking to ensure that everything cooks evenly and develops the desired grilling "crust."

3. Use direct heat (placing the food right over the heat) for meat and food that is smaller and requires less time (25 minutes or less). Use indirect heat (placing the food adjacent or near the heat source) for larger cuts of meat that should cook more slowly.

CHICKEN POT PIE MADE EASY

SERVINGS: 4–5

You can absolutely hit the easy button with this recipe for top-notch comfort food! Using rotisserie chicken and ready-to-bake biscuits from a can makes this classic dish so simple to throw together in a skillet. You get the same flaky topping, tender chicken and rich gravy with a lot less of the work. Yes, please.

If you have any pot pie leftovers, freeze that goodness in individual portions for another day! Same great dish, perfectly portable and reheatable for a delicious meal with zero work. See tip #7 in the introduction on page 16 for freezing recommendations.

2 tbsp (30 ml) olive oil

2 cups (220 g) diced carrot

1 cup (160 g) diced onion

½ tsp kosher salt

3 cups (336 g) shredded rotisserie chicken

1 cup (145 g) frozen peas, thawed

1 tsp dried thyme

4 tbsp (32 g) all-purpose flour

3 cups (720 ml) chicken stock

1 (16-oz [448-g]) can of biscuit dough

Preheat the oven to 400°F (204°C).

Heat the olive oil in a large, oven-proof 12-inch (30-cm) skillet over medium heat. When the pan feels hot, add the diced carrot, diced onion and kosher salt. Sauté for about 10 minutes, until the carrot is just soft enough to pierce with a fork.

Stir in the shredded chicken, peas, thyme and flour until everything is well incorporated. Pour in the chicken stock while whisking with a fork and bring the mixture to a low simmer. Cook for about 5 more minutes until the stock is slightly thickened.

Top the pot pie mixture with the raw biscuits and bake in the preheated oven for 15 minutes, until the biscuits are browned and cooked through.

Carefully remove the pan from the oven and let cool 5 minutes before serving.

TEEN CHEF TIP: Onions and carrots are the base for many dishes and soups, often also with diced celery. You can simplify this recipe and others by purchasing the mixture (called mirepoix) from the freezer section of many grocery stores. Alternatively, you can set aside a time to dice several onions and carrots, and then portion it out into smaller portions and freeze for your own homemade mirepoix mixtures. Simply remove it from the freezer and cook! If you don't allow time for the mixture to thaw, though, be ready to add a little extra time during the sauté step since you'll be starting with frozen vegetables.

EASY PORK FRIED RICE

SERVINGS: 4–5

Fried rice is sure to be a top contender for your go-to easy dinner that you can whip up with very little time and effort on a busy weeknight. You'll love how versatile fried rice can be—this recipe calls for pork, carrots, onion and frozen veggies, but you'll find after you've made it a few times that it's simple to substitute the protein and vegetables for what you have on hand. Instead of pork, you can try it with a chicken breast, thinly sliced flank steak, shrimp, etc. The rice you use is also customizable—you can use brown rice or white rice, jasmine or basmati (see the chef tip below for more recommendations about rice).

The secret to really great fried rice is high heat with short cook times. Each component is fried separately, then everything is stirred together at the end. Have fun with this recipe—you'll feel so profesh using your prep bowls, drizzling on the sauce and spices, and finally, plating up the crisp rice, tender veggies and flavorful meat!

4 cups (744 g) chilled cooked rice (see Teen Chef Tip)

1 lb (454 g) pork chops

2 tsp (5 g) granulated garlic, divided

1½ tsp (3 g) ground ginger, divided

1 tsp onion powder

3 tbsp (45 ml) soy sauce, divided, plus more to taste if needed

6 tbsp (90 ml) toasted sesame oil, divided

½ cup (80 g) yellow onion, finely diced

3 medium carrots, finely diced

1 cup (145 g) frozen peas, thawed

1 tsp butter

1 egg, beaten

Spread out your cooked rice on a plate to cool and dry out if needed (see Teen Chef Tip).

Cut the pork chops into thin 2-inch (5-cm) strips and place them in a small bowl. Season the pork strips with 1 teaspoon of garlic, 1 teaspoon of ginger and the onion powder. Stir in 2 tablespoons (30 ml) of soy sauce. Let the meat rest while you prepare your vegetables and heat the pan.

Heat a large 12-inch (30-cm) skillet over medium-high heat. When the pan feels hot (you can check by hovering your hand over it), add 2 tablespoons (30 ml) of the sesame oil. Place the seasoned pork in the hot oil in a flat layer and sauté for 2 to 3 minutes. Stir once and cook another 2 minutes. Transfer the cooked pork chops to a clean bowl (or a piece of parchment paper so you don't dirty another dish) and set aside.

Add 2 more tablespoons (30 ml) of sesame oil to the empty pan. Spread the diced onion and carrots in a flat layer in the pan. Season with 1 teaspoon of granulated garlic and ½ teaspoon of ground ginger. Sauté uncovered for 5 minutes. After 5 minutes, add a tablespoon (15 ml) of soy sauce and the peas to the carrots and onion, stir, and then spread the vegetables back into a flat layer. Cover the pan and cook for about 5 more minutes, until the carrots are tender.

Push the vegetables to the sides of the pan. Add the butter and then the beaten egg to the center of the pan. Let the egg cook for 1 minute, and then stir quickly to scramble the egg. Mix the egg and vegetables together well, and then remove them from the pan to rest in a clean bowl (or piece of parchment paper).

Add the final 2 tablespoons (30 ml) of sesame oil to the pan. Press the rice into the pan in a flat layer. Let the rice fry for 4 to 5 minutes.

Return the cooked meat and vegetables to the pan and stir well to incorporate. Serve with additional soy sauce as desired.

TEEN CHEF TIP: Fried rice is best with rice that is chilled, even better if it's a day or two old. Giving the rice time to dry out a bit and separate will result in a better final texture that isn't mushy or clumpy. A handy practice is next time you make rice fresh for a meal, make more than you need so you can make fried rice later in the week. If you don't have leftover rice, you can cook your rice first and then spread it out in a flat layer on a plate or baking sheet. Let the rice air out as long as you can, and if you have the time, you can stick it in the fridge. This is what I most often do because I don't usually have it ready ahead of time.

TATER TOT SUPREME

SERVINGS: 4-5

1 lb (454 g) ground sausage

1 (32-oz [896-g]) package tater tots

1 cup (240 ml) sour cream

1 cup (240 ml) barbecue sauce

2 cups (226 g) shredded cheese

1 cup (136 g) frozen yellow corn

OPTIONAL TOPPINGS
Additional barbecue sauce

Chopped green onion

Ranch dressing

When you're really in the mood for loaded potatoes, but you actually need a filling meal, this Tater Tot Supreme is the perfect solution! Crispy potatoes, melted cheese, creamy ranch—check. Add in crumbled sausage, sweet corn and barbecue sauce and you have a substantial dinner that really hits the spot!

Want to try something new? This recipe is also great for changing up the flavors and testing different variations. Swap ground beef for the sausage, sweet potato tots instead of regular or a new style of barbecue sauce. Keep these simple ingredients on hand for a quick tasty meal!

Preheat the oven to 400°F (204°C).

Heat a large, oven-proof skillet over medium heat. Add the ground sausage and sauté until the sausage is browned and cooked through. Drain any excess grease from the pan.

Add the tater tots and stir to incorporate the tots into the sausage. Stir together the sour cream, barbecue sauce and shredded cheese in a small mixing bowl or large liquid measuring cup. Pour the sauce mixture over the sausage and tot mixture and stir to mix it in well. Stir in the corn.

Transfer the skillet to the oven to bake for 25 minutes. (If you don't have an oven-safe skillet, transfer the tater tot mixture to an oven-safe pan, and then bake for 25 minutes.)

Serve hot with optional toppings as desired.

TEEN CHEF TIPS: When draining grease from a pan, never pour it directly down the drain. Instead, carefully pour it into a heat-safe dish and let the grease cool before discarding it in the trash. Another option is to keep a glass jar or metal can on hand to discard grease into. Store the jar in a cabinet or cover the metal can and tuck into the freezer. Once the jar or can is full, empty the grease into the trash can.

If you would like to make a simple barbecue sauce from scratch with staple ingredients, combine ½ cup (120 ml) ketchup, 2 tablespoons (30 ml) molasses, ¼ cup (40 g) minced yellow onion, 1 tablespoon (15 ml) apple cider vinegar and 1 tablespoon (15 ml) Worcestershire sauce in a small liquid measuring cup. Stir well, then pour the sauce into the tator tot mixture as stated in the recipe.

FANCY LASAGNA WITH NO LAYERING

SERVINGS: 6

Have you ever wanted to make a "fancy" meal that feels like a special occasion, but are turned off by the thought of all the extra work that comes with "fancy" dishes? Yeah, me too—which is why this Skillet Lasagna is the perfect "fancy" dinner hack! Lasagna may have a reputation for being complicated or time-consuming to make, but this recipe proves that it doesn't have to be.

This lasagna is prepared all in one skillet, no layering required, and tastes amazing! You won't miss the gooey cheesiness, the melt-in-your-mouth noodles, the hearty seasoned beef or the popping marinara sauce because it's all there! Just be sure to get no-boil lasagna noodles so you can stir them in to easily cook in the pan.

1 lb (454 g) ground beef

1 tbsp (5 g) dried oregano

1 tsp granulated garlic

1 tsp kosher salt

2 cups (60 g) fresh spinach leaves

2 (28-oz [784-g]) jars marinara sauce

8 oz (226 g) no-boil lasagna noodles

1 egg

16 oz (453 g) ricotta cheese

2 cups (224 g) shredded mozzarella cheese

1 cup (100 g) shredded Parmesan cheese

Preheat oven to 375°F (191°C).

Sauté the ground beef over medium heat in a 12-inch (30-cm) oven-proof skillet until the beef is crumbled and no longer pink. Drain any grease from the pan. Turn the heat to low. Add the oregano, garlic and salt to the browned meat, and then stir well to incorporate the seasonings. Stir in the spinach and marinara sauce.

Break the lasagna sheets into small pieces (roughly 2-inch [5-cm] pieces). Add the broken lasagna noodles to the skillet and stir well to incorporate. Make sure all the noodles are submerged in the sauce.

In a medium mixing bowl, stir together the egg, ricotta and mozzarella cheese. Dollop this cheese mixture into the skillet in several portions. Gently stir the cheese dollops into the lasagna mixture, just until there are no big clumps remaining.

Bake the lasagna skillet in the preheated oven for 30 minutes.

After 30 minutes, top the lasagna with the Parmesan cheese and bake for 5 more minutes until the Parmesan is melted and bubbly.

Carefully remove the lasagna from the oven and let it stand for 10 minutes before serving.

TEEN CHEF TIP: I am admittedly a tomato snob, and marinara sauce is not something I like to skimp on at the grocery store. A good marinara sauce will make a big difference in the overall flavor of your Italian dishes. Rao's brand is known to be one of the best you can get. Look for simple ingredients like tomatoes, oil, garlic and spices in your marinara.

One of my absolute favorite things to do in the summer is to buy fresh tomatoes (or grow them myself), and turn them into an amazing marinara sauce! You can use a variety of tomatoes to make marinara sauce, and even freeze any extra sauce to be enjoyed later on. Find a recipe for fresh summer marinara on my website: thispilgrimlife.com.

40   COOKING FROM SCRATCH FOR TEENS

THESE ARE CLASSICS FOR A REASON

There are some dishes that everyone should know how to make for themselves. They're delicious, nearly universally popular and well deserving of the timeless title "classic." A quick search online for "recipes everyone should know" will support my case. While there is some variation, there is more overlap and consensus on what qualifies as a must-know dish.

What might seem common or ordinary on paper can become extraordinary and mouth-watering when mastered at home—a savory burger, a tender omelet, a crisp from-scratch pizza, a perfectly seared steak. All are classics that you can learn to make at home for yourself, building up a catalog of recipes that will serve you for a lifetime.

The recipes in this chapter are varied but highly useful. Many of them are great for just making yourself a quick meal, or in the case of the Now & Later Spaghetti Bake (page 53), you can make one dish that you can eat right away as well as save for future meals.

There is even a recipe for homemade bread—a classic if there ever was one—with multiple variations. With this one recipe, you can make a loaf for dinner, sub rolls for sandwiches or sweet rolls for special treats. Fresh bread pairs perfectly with so many of the recipes in this book, so it's really convenient that you can make a loaf in just an hour!

THE BEST STEAK EVER

Learning to make your own steak at home, seasoned simply and cooked to perfection, is a monumental step in developing confidence and satisfaction in preparing your own food! Sure, a fancy meal in a nice steakhouse is a fun and enjoyable experience, but the reward of wowing your taste buds and impressing your family and friends lasts longer, not to mention saves you a lot of money.

This method is for reverse-searing ribeyes, which have marbling that yields a more flavorful steak. The goal of reverse searing is to slowly bring the steak up to temperature in the oven (just below the desired final temperature), before locking in the flavor by searing it in a hot pan. While this method takes a little longer, the benefits of a more even cook, an accurate temperature and better crust make it worthwhile. Pair this recipe with perfectly roasted garlic asparagus (page 84) for a dinner that will rival any restaurant!

3 cloves fresh garlic, peeled and smashed

3 tbsp (45 ml) olive oil, divided

1 lb (454 g) ribeye steak

½ tsp kosher salt

1 tsp fresh ground pepper

2 tbsp (28 g) butter (use a high-quality butter if possible, ideally grass-fed)

Preheat the oven to 275°F (135°C).

Wrap the smashed garlic and a tablespoon (15 ml) of olive oil in a small piece of foil. Place the foil packet in the oven to heat with the steak.

Rub the steak with 1 tablespoon (15 ml) of olive oil and then with the kosher salt and fresh ground pepper. Place the seasoned steak on a medium-sized baking sheet and put the baking sheet in the oven until the internal temperature of the steak reads 110°F (43°C) with a meat thermometer. This should take about 30 minutes if you start with a steak out of the fridge. Begin checking the temperature at about 20 minutes, and then in 5-minute intervals until it is ready.

When the steak's internal temperature reaches 110°F (43°C), remove the steak from the oven. Place a skillet on the stove and heat over medium-high heat. Add 1 tablespoon (15 ml) of olive oil. When the oil begins to smoke, add the butter and contents of the garlic packet. As soon as the butter foams, add the steak.

Sear the steak for 90 seconds per side, constantly spooning the garlic butter on top of the steak while it cooks. Hold the steak on its sides with a pair of tongs to cook for 20 seconds each side.

Remove the steak from the pan when the internal temperature reaches 130°F (54°C) and transfer it to a clean plate. Pour half the juice left in the skillet on top.

TEEN CHEF TIP: This method works best with a thick steak, at least 1½ inches (4 cm) thick. The times given in the recipe are to help give an idea of how long each step will take, but the most important indicator will be the internal temperature of the steak at each part in the process. An instant read meat thermometer is essential for a perfectly cooked steak. This recipe is for a steak cooked to medium-rare. If you want a more fully cooked steak, adjust the time slightly in the searing step.

KILLER FETTUCCINE ALFREDO

There's nothing quite like a bowl of hot pasta simply tossed with butter and cheese! In this authentic fettuccine alfredo, butter, Parmesan and the starchy pasta cooking liquid are all that are needed to add to your noodles, but you won't be wishing for anything else after you take your first bite! The absence of milk and cream is what makes this alfredo authentic. Because the butter and Parmesan are the primary components making up the flavor of this dish, you want to use the best options you can. A beautiful yellow, preferably grass-fed butter and freshly grated Parmesan (or a similar cheese like pecorino Romano) will make your pasta taste just like it's straight from the Italian countryside.

½ tsp kosher salt

½ lb (226 g) fettuccine or linguine noodles

1 cup (240 ml) reserved cooking liquid

4 tbsp (56 g) butter, cut into four pieces

1 cup (100 g) freshly grated Parmesan cheese

Bring 4 cups (960 ml) of water and the kosher salt to a boil. Add the pasta to the boiling water and boil for 8 minutes (follow the cooking time on the package).

Drain the pasta when it is tender and RESERVE the cooking liquid.

Transfer the cooked pasta to a bowl and stir in the butter, Parmesan and 1 cup (240 ml) of the reserved cooking liquid.

Taste and add additional cheese or salt according to preference.

TEEN CHEF TIP: When you add cheese to make a sauce, shred the cheese yourself rather than using bagged shredded cheese. Cheese that is pre-shredded is usually coated with an anti-caking agent to prevent the cheese from clumping up or sticking together. Unfortunately, this coating also makes it more difficult for the cheese to melt smoothly into a sauce. For a pasta dish like this one, using a good quality block of Parmesan cheese that's then grated by hand will result in a tastier dish.

SHARE-THE-LOVE COZY CHICKEN NOODLE SOUP

SERVINGS: 4–5

The next time you're under the weather or someone you care about is, make a batch of this soup! While all chicken noodle soup may be comforting when you're not feeling well, not every version will be equally beneficial. This particular recipe is packed with ingredients that are immunity boosting and nourishing to the body. Not only is the soup's broth nourishing and hydrating, it also helps to open up your airways and soothe a sore throat. The chicken provides your body with what it needs to feel restful and comforted, the vegetables supply important minerals and nutrients to support your immune system, and even the pasta is a helpful source of carbohydrate energy. Don't let its good-for-you-ness fool you, though. This soup is also incredibly delicious!

1 tsp kosher salt

½ tsp ground ginger

1 tsp turmeric

½ tsp dried thyme

½ tsp ground pepper

1 large chicken breast (approximately 1 lb [450 g])

2 tbsp (30 ml) olive oil

¼ cup (35 g) minced celery

½ cup (80 g) diced onion

1 cup (110 g) diced carrot

1 tbsp (9 g) minced garlic

6 cups (1.4 L) chicken stock

½ lb (226 g) pasta (a smaller variety like cavatelli or fusilli works best)

Grated Parmesan, for serving (optional)

In a small dish, stir together the kosher salt, ground ginger, turmeric, dried thyme and ground pepper. Pat the chicken breast dry, and season both sides with HALF of the spice mixture.

Heat a large soup pot or Dutch oven over medium heat. Add the olive oil when the pot is hot and then add the chicken. Brown the chicken breast on both sides for 3 minutes per side.

Push the chicken to the side of the pot and then add the chopped vegetables—minced celery, diced onion, diced carrot and minced garlic—to the center of the pot. Season the vegetables with the remaining spice mixture and stir. Sauté the vegetables for 5 minutes with no stirring.

Pour in the chicken stock, 2 cups (480 ml) of water and the pasta. Stir to combine and then bring the soup to a simmer. Simmer, partially covered, for 15 minutes, or until the pasta and the chicken are both cooked through.

Remove the chicken breast from the pot and shred it with two forks. Return the shredded chicken to the soup and stir to incorporate.

Taste and add additional salt as needed. If using, top with grated Parmesan to serve.

TEEN CHEF TIP: Homemade stock makes this soup even more nourishing and beneficial. You can easily make stock by simmering a chicken carcass in a pot of water with aromatics like onion, carrots and garlic. The mixture will impart nutrients and minerals to the water, creating a rich, flavorful stock that is better than anything you can get in the store. After a few hours of simmering, you can strain your stock and keep it in the fridge for up to 2 weeks or in the freezer for several months. For a full recipe on making homemade stock, visit my website, thispilgrimlife.com, for a crockpot or Instant Pot version.

SUPER EASY PIZZA WITH ENDLESS POSSIBILITIES

1⅓ cups (166 g) all-purpose flour, plus more for work surface

½ tsp sea salt

1 tsp active dry yeast

½ cup (120 ml) warm water, not exceeding 110°F (43°C)

½ cup (248 g) pizza sauce (see Teen Chef Tip)

1 cup (112 g) shredded mozzarella cheese

1 cup (weight varies) toppings of your choice (see Teen Chef Tip)

Do you have a favorite pizza combination? Have you ever tried replicating it yourself at home? This recipe for homemade pizza means you can have fun trying all kinds of different combinations of sauces and toppings!

Making the dough yourself doesn't need to be intimidating. I promise it's very easy to make, and it's also very quick—no long rise times, just a short rest while you prep your toppings. This recipe makes one pizza, but you can easily double or triple the recipe to make more pizzas. So, invite over a few friends and have a build-your-own pizza night! Just be sure to tell them it's BYOT—bring your own toppings!

Preheat the oven to 450°F (232°C).

In a medium-sized mixing bowl, combine the flour and sea salt. Stir to mix. In a liquid measuring cup, combine the yeast and the warm water. Let the yeast mixture stand for 3 minutes and then pour it into the bowl of flour. Stir the mixture together to form a soft dough.

Lightly dust your countertop with flour and transfer the dough to the counter to knead (press the dough, fold, rotate and repeat) until smooth. The surface of the dough should look uniform and no longer shaggy. Add a tablespoon (8 g) of flour at a time as needed if the dough sticks to your hands or the counter.

Grease a 10-inch (25-cm) pizza pan and then press the pizza dough into the pan until it reaches the edges, starting in the middle and evenly pressing it out. The dough should be thin and cover the entire pan.

Let the pizza dough rest on the pan for 10 minutes while you assemble the rest of your ingredients.

Once you've gathered your toppings, spread the sauce, then the mozzarella cheese and finally the toppings on the pizza. Bake in the preheated oven for 11 to 14 minutes, or until the crust is browned and the cheese is melted and bubbly.

Let the pizza rest at least 5 minutes before slicing.

TEEN CHEF TIP: The options for what you put on a homemade pizza are endless! Tomato-based pizza sauce or marinara sauce is an obvious option, but we also love using olive oil and spices, ranch dressing, pesto sauce and other sauces and dressings on our pizzas. Play around with different variations, and don't be afraid to try something simply because it's what you have on hand in the refrigerator. That's where great pizza discoveries are often made!

NOW & LATER SPAGHETTI BAKE

Transform basic spaghetti into a delicious and filling baked dinner and get double the payoff for your efforts! Spaghetti is already well known for being one of the easiest meal ideas when you're not sure what else to make, so tag this page as a go-to for dinner inspiration on the nights you know you're hungry but can't decide on a meal. This tasty twist on classic spaghetti incorporates mozzarella and Parmesan into the pasta, as well as eggs to hold everything together. Plus, part of the serious appeal of this dish is saving the leftovers for another day—that's one more day you won't have to figure out what's for dinner or dirty up any pans!

1 lb (454 g) spaghetti noodles

1 tbsp (15 ml) olive oil

1 lb (454 g) ground beef

1 tsp garlic powder

1 tsp oregano

½ tsp kosher salt

4 cups (960 g) marinara sauce

2 eggs, at room temperature

2 cups (224 g) shredded mozzarella cheese

1 cup (100 g) freshly grated Parmesan cheese

Preheat the oven to 350°F (177°C).

Break the spaghetti noodles in half and then cook the spaghetti in a large pot of boiling salted water for the time on the package directions. Drain the noodles in a colander and set them aside.

Drizzle a large skillet with olive oil, and then brown the ground beef until the beef crumbles and is no longer pink. Drain any grease from the pan. Season the ground beef with the garlic powder, oregano and kosher salt. Pour in the marinara sauce and stir. In a small bowl, whisk together the eggs and then add them to the meat mixture. Add the mozzarella cheese and then the cooked spaghetti noodles. Stir well.

Grease an 11 x 9-inch (30 x 23-cm) baking dish. Evenly spread the spaghetti mixture in the pan and smooth it into a flat layer. Top with the Parmesan cheese. Bake in the preheated oven for 20 minutes.

Cut leftover baked spaghetti into individual portions and freeze or refrigerate.

TEEN CHEF TIP

FIVE PRINCIPLES TO KNOW FOR COOKING PASTA

1. Use enough water to allow the noodles to move around freely as they cook. Some recipes, like the Killer Fettuccine Alfredo (page 46), may call for using a smaller amount of water to achieve a more concentrated, starchy liquid that you will use as a part of the final sauce.

2. Add salt to the pasta water. Cooking pasta in salted water will enhance the flavor of the pasta. Generally, you want to use about 1 tablespoon (18 g) of kosher salt per 4 quarts (3.8 L) of water.

3. Don't add oil to your pasta water, or the pasta after it drains. Oil will make your pasta slick so that the sauce cannot coat it as well.

4. Always add the pasta after the water starts boiling. Test the "doneness" of the pasta by taste.

5. Reserve part of the cooking liquid. You can use it to keep the pasta from clumping, add it to a sauce to thin it as needed, or even use it as a key part of the sauce (like in alfredo or carbonara).

EPIC MEAT LOVERS' CHILI

This chili is for the meat lovers—with both ground beef and stew meat, every bowl is bursting with hearty chunks of meat and deep chili flavor! People tend to hold strong opinions about chili, but this is a great recipe to get you started discovering your own chili preferences. There are endless additions and "secret tricks" to chili, so after you've tried this recipe a few times, put on your chef's hat and try a special tweak—maybe adding a spoonful of cocoa powder or a hot pepper or swapping the stew meat for sausage. The sky is the limit, but just be sure you record what you try so you'll know for the next time!

Heat a large Dutch oven or large pot over medium heat. Add 2 tablespoons (30 ml) of olive oil, then the ground beef and stew meat to the pot. Season the meat with 1 teaspoon of kosher salt and 1 teaspoon of chili powder. Sauté the meat, stirring occasionally, until it is all browned, about 10 to 15 minutes. Transfer the browned meat to a clean bowl with a slotted spoon. Discard any grease in the pot.

Add the remaining 2 tablespoons (30 ml) of olive oil to the center of the pot. Add the diced onions, diced peppers and minced garlic. Season the vegetables with 1 teaspoon of kosher salt, 2 teaspoons (3 g) of chili powder, smoked paprika, ground cumin and dried oregano. Stir to thoroughly incorporate the spices and then sauté the vegetables until they begin to soften, about 10 minutes.

When the vegetables are ready, return the meat to the pot. Add the diced tomatoes and beef stock. Bring the chili to a low simmer, then cook, simmering for at least 45 minutes, preferably 1 hour, until the stew meat is tender.

Taste and season the chili with any additional needed salt or, to add more heat, hot sauce or chili powder. Serve with optional toppings.

4 tbsp (60 ml) olive oil, divided

2 lb (908 g) ground beef

1 lb (454 g) stew meat

2 tsp (12 g) kosher salt, divided

3 tsp (5 g) chili powder, divided

2 yellow onions, diced

2 bell peppers, diced

2 tbsp (18 g) minced garlic

1 tsp smoked paprika

1 tsp ground cumin

2 tsp (4 g) dried oregano

2 (14-oz [414-ml]) cans diced tomatoes, undrained

1 (32-oz [946-ml]) carton beef stock

OPTIONAL TOPPINGS
Sour cream

Fresh diced tomatoes

Cheddar cheese

Hot sauce

TEEN CHEF TIP: A good chili shouldn't be rushed. The chili needs to simmer for a while to give the meat time to become tender, and for the flavors to develop well throughout. Moreover, chili is often better the second day, so if you want an even tastier chili, make it a day early!

HOMESTYLE BAKED MAC 'N' CHEESE

If you're anything like I was, you could live off mac 'n' cheese—especially mac 'n' cheese topped with crumbled, buttery crackers. The combination was one of my most frequent easy dinners as a college student. This Homestyle Baked Mac 'n' Cheese is a nod to those college days and is perfect for your own cheesy pasta cravings! Tender macaroni noodles in a creamy cheese sauce, with a crisp, buttery topping—it's worth the extra effort, perfect for holidays, tasty steak dinners or regular weekdays.

½ lb (226 g) elbow macaroni noodles

2 tbsp (28 g) butter

2 tbsp (16 g) all-purpose flour

2 cups (480 ml) whole milk

½ tsp kosher salt

½ tsp dry mustard powder

1½ cups (170 g) shredded extra sharp Cheddar cheese

TOPPING
10 butter crackers, crumbled

2 tbsp (28 g) melted butter

¼ cup (28 g) shredded Cheddar cheese

¼ tsp paprika

Preheat oven to 350°F (177°C).

Boil the elbow macaroni in 4 cups (960 ml) of water according to package directions. Drain.

In a medium-sized pot, melt the butter over medium heat. When the butter is completely melted, whisk in the flour, and then gradually whisk in the milk. Heat the milk until it is beginning to bubble on the surface and is thicker, whisking almost constantly. Stir in the salt, dry mustard and Cheddar cheese. Remove the pot from the heat.

Grease an 8 x 8–inch (20 x 20–cm) square baking dish and then add the cooked macaroni to the dish. Pour in the cheese mixture and stir until all the noodles are evenly coated.

Stir together the butter crackers, melted butter, Cheddar cheese and paprika in a small bowl with a fork. Spread the mixture on the cheesy noodles, and then bake uncovered for 20 minutes.

TEEN CHEF TIP: If you need to reheat a pasta dish, you can add a little extra liquid to prevent the noodles from drying out. For a pasta with a creamy sauce like this, simply heat with a few tablespoons (45 ml) of milk and a pinch more of salt. For other dishes, a little butter melted in a pan is a great way to bring leftover pasta back to life.

SLIDERS WITH AN UPGRADE

SERVINGS: 4-6

Do you want to know the EASIEST way to make burgers at home? It's making sliders! No need to fire up the grill, and (trust me here) no need to even mix together seasoned burger patties. These sliders are knock-your-socks-off delicious, and all you do is press the meat into the pan, top with a savory homemade burger sauce and bake! That's it!

These Sliders with an Upgrade are an umami-rich version of my classic slider. The salty Swiss cheese perfectly complements the buttery sautéed mushrooms. You can cut these into single patties or stack them for a double cheeseburger. Pair these with the Homemade Potato Chip Dip (page 130) for an exceptionally tasty burger night!

1 lb (454 g) ground beef

1 tbsp (15 ml) Worcestershire sauce

1 tbsp (15 ml) soy sauce

1 tsp granulated onion

1½ tsp (4 g) granulated garlic, divided

3 cups (210 g) sliced mushrooms

7 tbsp (98 g) butter, divided

6 slices Swiss cheese

6 hamburger buns

½ tsp kosher salt

Preheat the oven to 375°F (191°C).

Press the ground beef in a flat layer in a 9 x 11-inch (23 x 28-cm) baking dish, leaving a 1-inch (2.5-cm) border around the pan—the meat shouldn't extend across the entire pan. In a small dish, stir together the Worcestershire sauce, soy sauce, granulated onion and 1 teaspoon of the granulated garlic. Evenly spread the sauce across the top of the ground beef with a spatula.

Bake the sliders in the preheated oven for 25 minutes.

While the sliders are cooking, melt 3 tablespoons (42 g) of butter in a small pan over low heat. Then add and sauté the mushrooms until softened and slightly caramelized, 5 to 10 minutes.

After the baking time is complete, turn off the oven, remove the pan and drain most of the grease from the pan. Top the large patty with the sliced Swiss cheese, evenly spreading the cheese across the top. Return the pan to the now-turned-off oven to melt.

Prepare the burger buns by spreading the remaining 4 tablespoons (56 g) of butter on the insides of the bun and sprinkling them with the kosher salt and remaining ½ teaspoon of granulated garlic. After the cheese is melted on the patty, remove the pan from the oven. Place the prepared buns in the oven, butter side up, either on a baking sheet or directly on the oven rack. Use the broil function to toast the buns for 3 to 5 minutes (watch them closely so they don't burn).

Divide the sliders in the pan into 6 equal portions. Assemble the sliders with the toasted buns, topping the patty with a heap of sautéed mushrooms. Alternately, you can make a double burger by layering two sliders together.

TEEN CHEF TIP: This recipe doubles very well and is a great opportunity to work smarter, not harder and freeze individual burger patties after they are cooked. Wrap them in foil and freeze in a zipper freezer bag. Reheat in the oven at 350°F (177°C) until they are hot and have a burger whenever you want!

AMAZING HOMEMADE BREAD IN 1 HOUR (FRENCH, SUB ROLLS & CINNAMON RAISIN BUNS)

SERVINGS: 4–6

FRENCH BREAD OR SUB ROLLS

3½ cups (480 g) bread flour, divided, plus more for work surface

1½ tsp (9 g) sea salt

1 tbsp (12 g) active dry yeast

1½ cups (360 ml) warm water, not exceeding 110°F (43°C)

1 egg

Making soft bread from scratch (with yeast!) puts you on the fast track to feeling like a real home chef! Working with dough can be such a relaxing and calming activity. Baking bread makes your house smell like an amazing bakery, and as if that wasn't enough, enjoying a warm slice with a thick slab of butter and a sprinkle of coarse salt is absolutely one of life's greatest pleasures.

This recipe is reliable and easy, making it a great recipe for anyone learning to make homemade bread. I've included three variations in the recipe: (1) bake a single French loaf, (2) divide the dough to make sub rolls and (3) use the base plus a handful of other ingredients to make a dozen sweet cinnamon raisin buns.

TO MAKE FRENCH BREAD

Preheat the oven to 200°F (93°C) and then turn it off when it reaches 200°F (93°C).

In a medium-sized mixing bowl, combine 3 cups (375 g) of flour and the sea salt. In a liquid measuring cup, combine the yeast and warm water. Gently stir the yeast mixture and then pour it into the bowl of flour and salt. Stir with a wooden spoon until the mixture is soft and the flour is completely incorporated. Stir in the remaining ½ cup (63 g) of flour.

Transfer the mixture to a lightly floured countertop and knead the dough by pressing down with the heel of your hand, folding the dough in half, rotating it 90 degrees and repeating the pressing, folding and rotating process. Work the dough, adding extra flour whenever the counter or dough is sticky, until you have a smooth ball of dough.

(continued)

FRENCH BREAD PHOTO STEPS

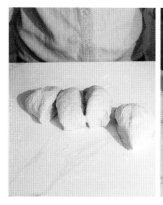   

AMAZING HOMEMADE BREAD IN 1 HOUR (CONT.)

Lightly dust your countertop with flour again, and then press the dough into a 10 x 12-inch rectangle. Roll the dough into a tight log and place it on a baking sheet lined with parchment paper. Loosely cover the bread with a lightweight dishtowel or cloth napkin. Place the tray in the warm oven to rise for 10 minutes.

After 10 minutes, remove the tray from the oven and heat the oven to 425°F (218°C). Let the bread continue to rise, covered, on the stove or near the oven while it heats.

Beat the egg in a small bowl and then brush the loaf of bread with the beaten egg just before you bake it.

Bake the bread in the hot oven for 18 to 20 minutes, until the bread is golden brown on top. Let the bread cool at least 15 minutes before slicing.

TO MAKE SUB ROLLS

Follow the directions above, except divide the dough into four portions. Press each portion into an 8-inch (20-cm) square and roll it into a tight log. Lay each roll next to each other on a lined baking sheet.

Loosely cover the sub rolls with a lightweight dishtowel or cloth napkin. Place the tray in the warm oven to rise for 10 minutes.

After 10 minutes, remove the tray from the oven and heat the oven to 425°F (218°C). Let the bread continue to rise, covered, on the stove or near the oven while it heats.

Beat the egg in a small bowl and then brush the sub rolls with the beaten egg just before you bake it.

Bake in the preheated oven for 14 to 16 minutes, until the rolls are golden brown on top. Let the sub rolls cool at least 15 minutes before slicing.

(continued)

CINNAMON RAISIN BUNS PHOTO STEPS

TO MAKE CINNAMON RAISIN BUNS

In a medium-sized mixing bowl, combine 3 cups (375 g) of flour and the sea salt. Stir in the cinnamon, nutmeg and sugar. In a liquid measuring cup, combine the yeast and warm water. Gently stir the yeast mixture, then pour it into the bowl of dry ingredients. Stir with a wooden spoon until the flour is completely incorporated and the mixture is soft. Stir in the raisins and remaining ½ cup (63 g) of flour.

Transfer the mixture to a lightly floured countertop and knead the dough by pressing down with the heel of your hand, folding the dough in half, rotating it 90 degrees, and repeating the pressing, folding and rotating process. Work the dough, adding extra flour whenever the counter or dough is sticky, until you have a smooth ball.

After kneading the dough, divide it into 12 equal portions (3 to 4 ounces [85 to 113 g] each). Cover the dough with a lightweight towel or cloth napkin while it rests for 10 minutes.

In a small bowl, stir together the softened butter, brown sugar and cinnamon. Press each of the 12 portions of dough into a small rectangle and spread on some of the sweet butter mixture. Roll each little rectangle up and tuck into a greased muffin tray.

Let the cinnamon raisin buns rise near/on the oven while you heat it to 400°F (204°C).

Bake the buns in the hot oven for 15 minutes.

Make a simple glaze by mixing together the powdered sugar with 1 tablespoon (15 ml) water. Drizzle the glaze over the cooled cinnamon raisin buns.

TEEN CHEF TIP: Bread flour is flour that has a higher protein content that produces more gluten than an all-purpose flour. The gluten is what gives bread the chewy, stretchy quality. I like to use it for loaves of bread, and especially in recipes where I am speeding up the rising time. Bread flour will rise better and more quickly, making it ideal for quick breads.

AMAZING HOMEMADE BREAD IN 1 HOUR (CONT.)

CINNAMON RAISIN BUNS
3½ cups (480 g) bread flour, divided, plus more for work surface

1½ tsp (9 g) sea salt

1½ tsp (4 g) ground cinnamon, divided

¼ tsp ground nutmeg

2 tbsp (30 g) granulated sugar

1 tbsp (12 g) active dry yeast

1½ cups (360 ml) warm water, not exceeding 110°F (43°C)

1 cup (145 g) raisins

CINNAMON-SUGAR FILLING
¼ cup (56 g) butter, room temperature

2 tbsp (28 g) brown sugar

½ tsp ground cinnamon

GLAZE
¾ cup (90 g) powdered sugar

1 tbsp (15 ml) water, or more to get your desired consistency

PERFECT LATE-NIGHT OMELET

SERVINGS: 1

There's something about nighttime that makes you extra hungry, but who wants to do much cooking late at night? Omelets are your answer to an empty stomach after the sun has (long since) gone down. They're filling and tasty, while still being easy to prepare. The next time you're coming home late from work or hanging out with friends and desperate for a quick bite to eat before crashing in bed, remember these perfect omelets.

Omelets can seem a little tedious when you first make them. And it's true, they can be. Once you make them a few times, though, you figure out what makes them work and you forget about their finickiness. Enjoy an omelet plain or add your favorite fillings like cheese, crumbled bacon, sautéed mushrooms—whatever you like!

2 eggs

1 tsp water

1½ tsp (7 g) butter

Pinch of kosher salt

OPTIONAL
¼ cup (weight varies) total of your favorite toppings, such as shredded cheese, sautéed vegetables and/or crumbled bacon

TEEN CHEF TIP: This recipe calls for adding water, not milk, to the eggs. This helps to ensure a light and fluffy omelet because instead of weighing the eggs down, the water creates steam and lift as the eggs cook. In scrambled eggs, milk is preferred to result in rich and creamy eggs.

Set an 8-inch (20-cm) non-stick or cast-iron pan on the stove over medium heat.

In a small bowl, whisk together the eggs and the water, until the eggs are quite uniform and starting to get frothy.

Add the butter to the pan. Once the butter is melted and just begins to bubble, pour in the whisked eggs. Gently move the eggs around in the pan until they are almost completely cooked, trying to keep them mostly flat across the bottom of the pan. This should take a minute and a half (setting a stopwatch can help avoid overcooking the eggs).

Once the eggs are mostly cooked, use your spatula to gently spread them to a uniform layer, pushing any uncooked eggs out to the edges of the pan.

Remove the pan from the heat, sprinkle with a pinch of kosher salt and add any topping(s) across the top of the eggs. Use your spatula to roll your omelet, tilting the pan to help it roll onto itself.

Transfer to a plate and enjoy immediately.

EAT YOUR VEGGIES

I'm going to let you in on a secret I wish I had learned sooner—vegetables are powerhouses of flavor. When prepared properly, they can be THE THING that makes a meal sing. Pickled, roasted, sautéed or simply eaten fresh with a little salt—the potential is endless.

Not only that, but vegetables are really good for you. I know, I'm not revealing anything mysterious with that statement. Obvious as it may be though, it's true that "eating the rainbow" is an important part of a healthy lifestyle. Find some vegetables you love and work them regularly into your diet. Then, keep trying new vegetables and new ways to prepare them because it can take several exposures to new foods before we develop a taste for them.

My mission in this chapter is to highlight how tasty vegetables are, as well as to make it easy and convenient to enjoy them often. Make the Awesome Caesar Salad Wraps (page 72) and enjoy a delicious hand-held salad wherever your plans take you. Use the recipe for Mexican Street Corn Made Easy (page 71) as a flavorful side dish or even as a topping for your Crazy Delicious Hot Dog Bar (page 129). Or, simply blend up a batch of Energy-Boosting Green Smoothie (page 79) for a fast, vitamin-rich pick-me-up whenever you need it!

MEXICAN STREET CORN MADE EASY

SERVINGS: 6

Selecting a side dish to serve with Tex-Mex or Mexican dishes can be a challenge, but this skillet street corn is a total no-brainer! Traditional Mexican street corn is served whole on the cob, grilled and charred, then finished with a creamy, spicy sauce and a dusting of salty cheese. It's so flavorful and delicious!

This skillet version simplifies the process of making street corn (you're welcome), while keeping the same essential components and flavors. Kernels of corn are charred in a skillet, tossed with a homemade sauce, and then stirred together with Cotija cheese and slices of green onion. Serve it as an amazing side dish for tacos or enchiladas, or even as a delicious hot dog topping (page 129)!

1 tbsp (15 ml) ghee or cooking oil

1 (16-oz [454-g]) bag frozen yellow corn, thawed

¼ cup (60 ml) mayonnaise

¼ cup (60 ml) Greek yogurt

2 tbsp (30 ml) lime juice

1 tsp chili powder

½ cup (60 g) Cotija cheese

2 green onion stalks, both the white and green, chopped

Cilantro, for topping

Heat a skillet over medium heat. Add the ghee, swirl it to cover the bottom of the pan and then add the corn. Spread the corn out into a flat layer and sauté for 10 minutes. Stir the corn once after 5 minutes, then spread it back into a flat layer. The corn should char slightly in the pan. Cook for another 5 minutes.

While the corn cooks, stir together the mayonnaise, Greek yogurt, lime juice and chili powder to make the dressing in a liquid measuring cup. After the corn has been in the pan about 10 minutes, remove it from the heat, then stir in the dressing, Cotija cheese and sliced green onion.

Serve with fresh cilantro for topping.

TEEN CHEF TIP: Layers of flavor, varying textures and a mix of cooked and fresh ingredients make dishes interesting and give them more depth. This dish works well with the heat and tang of the sauce, saltiness of the cheese and crisp flavors of the green onion and cilantro. If you want to take your food to the next level, pay attention to how you can include complementary flavors and textures.

AWESOME CAESAR SALAD WRAPS

Trying to pack salad to go can be inconvenient. You need a container for the salad, a smaller container for the dressing to pour over just before eating and don't forget a fork or you'll be eating with your fingers. Then bring it all back home. Salad wraps are a convenient solution—no need for containers or forks, so no forgetting dirty containers in your car for weeks.

These Caesar salad wraps are so crisp and refreshing! Using chicken nuggets from the freezer makes them more filling and smashing the croutons before wrapping helps keep everything neatly together. They're a perfect picnic food for a sunny day at the park or to pack for an easy, healthy lunch at school. Check out the Teen Chef Tips below for more salad wrap ideas!

4 cups (140 g) finely chopped romaine lettuce

2 cups (280 g) chopped chicken nuggets

1 cup (240 ml) Caesar dressing

1 heaping cup (30 g) croutons

6 (8-inch [20-cm]) flour tortillas

Mix together the lettuce, chicken and Caesar dressing. Stir well to coat everything with the dressing.

Place the croutons in a sandwich bag and smash with the back of a spoon or bottom of a measuring cup. Stop when the croutons are mostly crumbled. Add the crushed croutons to the bowl of salad mix and stir to incorporate.

Measure out 1 cup (240 ml) of the salad mixture onto the center of a tortilla. Fold in the sides of the tortilla and then holding the sides in place, roll the tortilla into a tight log. Repeat with the five remaining tortillas.

Eat immediately or refrigerate the salad wraps for 2 to 3 days.

TEEN CHEF TIP: You can use this same method of making salad wraps to enjoy all kinds of variations of your favorite salads. Simply mix together your ingredients in a bowl and add a little more dressing than you would if you were eating the salad on a plate—the extra dressing boosts the flavor and keeps it from tasting dry after being wrapped in a tortilla. Making sure each of the components is roughly the same size will help your wrap stay together better and make every bite a perfect combination of elements.

A FEW WRAP IDEAS TO GET YOU STARTED

- Everyone's Favorite Tuna Salad (page 97) + crunchy romaine lettuce + a dollop of Greek yogurt + a drop of Dijon mustard
- Leftover steak (page 45) + spring mix + a thinly sliced tomato & bell pepper + Greek dressing
- Canned wild salmon (drained) + arugula + avocado chunks + halved cherry tomatoes + a dollop of mayo + a sprinkle of lemon juice + a pinch of kosher salt

HIKER'S SALAD WITH CREAMY CITRUS POPPYSEED DRESSING

If you're on the fence about salad, or simply needing some fresh inspiration to enjoy new kinds of salad, you should definitely put this salad on your list of recipes to try soon! This salad is crunchy trail mix meets bed of tender lettuce, with a sweet and tangy dressing drizzled on top. It's such a fun salad to enjoy with fresh and dried fruit, nuts and seeds—you'll be coming back for more and more!

Add the salad greens, followed by the sliced red apple, craisins, sunflower seeds and sliced almonds to a plate or salad bowl.

In a pint-sized jar, combine the mayonnaise, orange juice, honey, poppy seeds, kosher salt and Dijon mustard to make the dressing and stir well with a fork, or mix together by shaking the jar.

Drizzle the salad dressing over the top of the salad (according to your preference).

Keep the dressing covered in the refrigerator for up to 2 weeks.

SALAD

2 cups (100 g) mixed salad greens

¼ cup (31 g) sliced red apple

3 tbsp (22 g) craisins

2 tbsp (16 g) lightly salted sunflower seeds

2 tbsp (14 g) sliced almonds

DRESSING

1 cup (240 ml) mayonnaise

3 tbsp (45 ml) orange juice

2 tbsp (30 ml) honey

2 tsp (6 g) poppy seeds

1 tsp kosher salt

½ tsp Dijon mustard

TEEN CHEF TIP: Homemade salad dressings are so easy to make! You can make simple vinaigrettes with olive oil and vinegar, or creamy dressings with mayonnaise and/or yogurt. With the base in place, you can make any kind of dressing by varying the spices and herbs, sweeteners and so on. Topping your salads with homemade dressings can give them an extra fresh and flavorful taste—plus, you can save money and skip unnecessary ingredients or extra sugars.

SWEET & SAVORY VEGGIE SOUP

Need a hot lunch that is easy to make and even easier to eat? Smooth, blended soups are a great lunch option—enjoy a bowl of soup with a biscuit or quesadilla on the side for dipping, or pour a cup of soup in a mug or thermos for sipping while you're sitting at your desk or driving in the car.

This carrot and apple soup is both sweet and savory and is finished with a tangy yogurt drizzle. You can add salted, roasted pumpkin or sunflower seeds for an added crunch, but don't let the simplicity of this soup fool you—it's delicious!

1 tbsp (14 g) ghee

½ cup (80 g) diced yellow onion

4 cups (512 g) diced carrot

2 apples, peeled and cubed

½ tsp kosher salt

½ tsp ground ginger

4 cups (480 ml) chicken stock

HONEY YOGURT DRIZZLE
½ cup (120 ml) plain whole milk yogurt

2 tsp (10 ml) honey

Heat a medium-sized soup pot or Dutch oven over medium heat. Add the ghee and then once the pot is hot, add the diced onion and sauté for 5 minutes until the onion begins to soften and turn translucent. Stir in the carrot, apples, kosher salt, ground ginger and chicken stock.

Bring the soup mixture to a low simmer and cook for 20 minutes, until the carrot is fork tender.

Use an immersion blender to blend the soup, or carefully transfer the hot soup to a blender and blend.

Stir together the yogurt and honey and then lightly drizzle it over the bowls of soup.

TEEN CHEF TIPS: An immersion blender is a helpful tool for blending soups and sauces right in the bowl or pot in which they're made. Start on the lowest speed and then build up to the fastest speed until the soup is completely blended. If you prefer an even smoother soup, you can carefully transfer the soup to a blender to blend.

Making your own chicken stock is an awesome way to boost the overall flavor of your food, besides adding extra nutrition and saving money! All you need are chicken bones (preferably an entire carcass from a roasted or rotisserie chicken) and some simple additions to add flavor. In a slow cooker, large pot or electric pressure cooker, cover the bones with water, and add two diced carrots, a quartered onion, a couple of halved garlic cloves, several peppercorns and a pinch of dried thyme. A splash of apple cider vinegar can also help to draw out more nutrients. For a slow cooker, heat the mixture on low heat for 8 to 10 hours. For a stockpot on the stove, bring the liquid to a low simmer and cook for 2 to 3 hours. For an electric pressure cooker, cook the mixture for 60 minutes on high pressure (not exceeding the fill line). Once your stock is ready, simply strain and discard all but the liquid. Use it or freeze it within a week.

ENERGY-BOOSTING GREEN SMOOTHIE

I know it can be tempting to automatically turn to caffeine or sugar when you feel like you need a pick-me-up or a boost in energy. Been there. Hear me out, though. Feeling sluggish and tired is a signal from your body to replenish it with the fuel it craves! The first and easiest solution is always drinking a glass of water. Next, try this green smoothie to give your body the vitamins and nutrients you need. All the veggies and fruit in this smoothie give it a bright, fresh taste and make it an instant energy and mood booster! Try it as a mid-morning or afternoon snack the next time you need a little extra energy.

¼ cucumber, peeled

¼–½ cup (60–120 ml) orange juice (see Note)

1 rib celery

1½ handfuls spinach

½ cup (120 g) frozen avocado (look for it in the freezer section of your local grocery store)

½ apple, peeled & cored

½ cup (120 g) ice

Combine the cucumber, orange juice, celery, spinach, avocado, apple and ice in a blender and blend the ingredients until the mixture is smooth. If you prefer a thinner smoothie, add water to thin the smoothie until it is your desired consistency.

Pour half of the smoothie into a glass for a full serving now, and the second half into a jar with a lid to save in the fridge to be enjoyed within a few days. Or, you can divide it into smaller portions for more people or days.

NOTE: You can determine how much orange juice to use according to your preference. A ½ cup (120 ml) of orange juice will result in a sweeter smoothie. If you prefer less sugar in your smoothie, you can use ¼ cup (60 ml) of juice and ¼ cup (60 ml) of water instead.

TEEN CHEF TIP: You can prep extra green smoothie packets to keep in the freezer to make green smoothies even easier! Combine all the ingredients in a quart-sized (960 ml) freezer bag (you can freeze orange juice in an ice cube tray too). With this option, you can also use fresh ripe avocado rather than the precut frozen kind since it will get frozen with the rest of the mix. To make a smoothie with the frozen packets, add ½ cup (120 ml) of water to the blender first to get the blending started and then just blend until smooth.

UNBELIEVABLY DELICIOUS VEG TART

SERVINGS: 6-8

You'll feel extra fancy serving this special appetizer, but it's actually quite simple to make! Vegetables bursting with flavor, a creamy ranch sauce and puff pastry come together for an amazingly delicious dish! Serve the tart as an appetizer for a special dinner or as part of a tasty lunch spread. Try it with the vegetables roasted and fresh and see which you prefer.

1 cup (149 g) grape tomatoes, sliced in half

1 bell pepper, sliced into strips

2 green onions, chopped & green tops reserved

1 tbsp (15 ml) olive oil

1 sheet of frozen puff pastry, thawed

SAUCE

4 oz (112 g) cream cheese, room temperature

4 tbsp (56 g) butter, melted

½ tsp kosher salt

½ tsp onion powder

½ tsp granulated garlic

½ tsp dill

1 tsp parsley

½ cup (50 g) shredded Parmesan cheese

Preheat the oven to 400°F (204°F). Spread the tomatoes, bell pepper and the white parts of the green onions out on a baking tray. Lightly drizzle the vegetables with olive oil and place the tray in the oven while it heats and you prepare your pastry. Set a timer for 10 minutes.

Roll out the puff pastry onto your baking sheet or pizza tray. To make the pastry a round shape for a pizza tray, trim off the overhanging pieces and cut them to fit into the open spaces on the tray. Overlap the edges slightly and press gently to secure. In a small bowl, stir together the cream cheese, butter, kosher salt, onion powder, granulated garlic, dill and parsley until everything is well combined and smooth.

Spread the cream sauce on the puff pastry, leaving a 1-inch (2.5-cm) border around the sides. Use a pair of tongs to transfer the vegetables to the pastry.

Bake the vegetable tart for 10 minutes in the preheated oven.

When the baking time is complete, top the tart with the Parmesan cheese and reserved green onion tops. Let the tart cool for 10 minutes before slicing and transferring to a serving plate.

TEEN CHEF TIP: Save the roots of your green onions! You can put a green onion root (with 1 inch [2.5 cm] left of the white stem) in a jar with a cup of water, set them in a sunny spot and watch them grow back. Give the green onions fresh water every few days and peel off the outer sheath if it gets slimy. They'll be ready to enjoy again in just a week or two!

PASTA & VEGGIE SOUP TO FILL YOU UP

SERVINGS: 4-5

If you love the flavor of caramelized onions, or enjoy savory soups, then this soup is for you! Minestrone is a classic Italian vegetable soup that is a filling and hearty, thanks to the beans and the pasta. This version starts by building a rich flavor with caramelized onions, then saves time by using a simple blend of frozen vegetables—I like using a mix of green beans, carrots, corn and peas. Pair this soup with a loaf of homemade French bread (page 61) for a nutritious and satisfying meal!

2 tbsp (28 g) butter

1 yellow onion, diced

1½ tsp (9 g) kosher salt, divided

1 tbsp (16 g) tomato paste

1 tbsp (15 ml) Worcestershire sauce

4 cups (960 ml) beef stock

2 cups (480 ml) water

2 cups (480 ml) tomato sauce

1 (14-oz [414-ml]) can cannellini beans, drained & rinsed

2 cups (168 g) small pasta

3 cups (405 g) frozen mixed vegetables, thawed

1 cup (100 g) grated Parmesan cheese

Heat a Dutch oven or large soup pot over medium heat. Melt the butter and then add the diced onion. Sprinkle ½ teaspoon of kosher salt over the onion. Sauté the onion for 10 minutes, stirring once, until it is browned and softened.

Add the tomato paste and Worcestershire sauce to the onion. Stir the paste and sauce into the onion, scraping up anything stuck to the bottom of the pot.

Pour in the beef stock, water, tomato sauce and remaining 1 teaspoon of kosher salt. Stir in the beans and pasta. Bring the soup to a simmer.

Simmer the soup for 10 minutes, until the pasta is al dente. Add the mixed vegetables and return the soup to a simmer. Simmer for 5 more minutes.

Taste and season the soup with additional salt as needed. Serve the soup with grated Parmesan cheese on top.

TEEN CHEF TIP: Soup that has pasta or rice in it can continue to absorb the broth the longer it sits, which means leftovers often seem less like soup and more like a casserole. To enjoy leftovers, you can add additional broth when you warm the soup (you will need to add additional salt for flavor) or consider your leftover soup a fresh new meal and heat it with some butter in a pan.

PERFECT ROASTED VEGETABLES

If you think you don't like a vegetable, try it roasted before you write it off completely! Roasting vegetables is one of the most convenient and reliable ways to ensure great tasting vegetables. Not much is needed—just a little fat, salt, simple seasoning and a hot oven.

Three of the best and easiest vegetables to roast are carrots, broccoli and asparagus. Give the carrots a little spicy kick and cut them as fries—they're delicious dipped in ranch! Broccoli is incredible roasted until charred and crisp, then topped with a light coating of Parmesan cheese. Asparagus is perfect topped with generous heaps of fresh garlic and roasted until tender. Pick one to roast for dinner or roast all three in a row on a large baking sheet.

Preheat the oven to 425°F (218°C).

Spread the vegetables in a flat layer on a rimmed baking sheet. Drizzle the vegetables with olive oil, and then add the kosher salt and spices. Give the baking sheet a little shake to mix.

Roast the vegetables in the preheated oven for 12 to 15 minutes until the vegetables are tender and slightly blackened, giving the vegetables a little stir or giving the tray a little shake halfway through.

Top the broccoli with the Parmesan cheese.

CARROTS
8 carrots, peeled and sliced into thin spears

3 tbsp (45 ml) olive oil

½ tsp kosher salt

½ tsp chili powder

½ tsp granulated garlic

¼ tsp turmeric

BROCCOLI
1 head broccoli, florets sliced in half

3 tbsp (45 ml) olive oil

½ tsp kosher salt

½ tsp oregano

½ tsp fresh ground pepper

½ cup (50 g) shredded Parmesan cheese, for topping

ASPARAGUS
1 bunch asparagus, woody bottoms removed

2 tbsp (30 ml) olive oil

½ tsp kosher salt

½ tsp fresh ground pepper

¼ cup (34 g) minced garlic

TEEN CHEF TIP

HOW TO HOLD A CHEF'S KNIFE: For better control while you cut vegetables (or other foods), firmly pinch the knife just above the handle with your index finger and thumb, and then wrap your other three fingers around the handle. Having your hand a little bit closer to the tip will allow you to make more controlled slices and cuts. With your other hand, hold the vegetables in place, but tuck your fingers under to form a claw shape, keeping them out of the way of the knife.

HUNGRY AGAIN? SNACKS THAT SATISFY

Teenagers have a reputation of "eating you out of house and home." That may be true, but it's not without good reason. It's a teenager's job to grow and eat and eat and grow.

The trick is knowing how to snack well by eating proteins, whole grains and healthy fats. If you include these in your daily diet, you will find yourself snacking in a way that fills you up, meaning fewer trips back and forth to the kitchen, so you can focus on doing other things and maybe your parents can sweat the grocery bill a little less!

As an expert snacker myself, I know spending a lot of time making complicated snacks is not ideal. If the recipe is too involved, I'll just resort to something else (often empty calories that perpetuate that endless snack cycle). So, I made sure to include recipes in this chapter that do not require long preparations or cook times. Better-for-You Instant Ramen (page 89) is a healthier alternative to cheap packages of ramen noodles that you can make on the stovetop in about ten minutes. Everyone's Favorite Tuna Salad (page 97) is so simple to prepare but also a completely satisfying snack.

A few of the recipes are easy to make and freeze for future snack cravings. Ridiculously Good Ham Sliders (page 98), Awesome Black Bean Taquitos (page 101) and Take-Anywhere Energy Bites (page 102) all keep well in the freezer, ready to be reheated or enjoyed as is when you need them.

BETTER-FOR-YOU INSTANT RAMEN

Making savory ramen noodles from scratch is super fast and convenient. You won't miss the packaged seasoning packets with simple additions like flavorful stock, soy sauce and common spices. You still get a delicious, filling afternoon snack, plus a little nutrition, too.

If you want to have a little fun testing flavors and experimenting with different ingredients, this is a great recipe to play with. You'll feel like a true home chef without much effort! My teen son Jack helped develop this recipe and loves to add sliced mushrooms and a pinch of ginger to his bowl. You can enjoy the simplicity of the noodles and savory stock or try out different variations by adding in soft boiled eggs, mushrooms, Sriracha, bean sprouts and more.

1½ cups (360 ml) beef stock or broth

1 ramen cake (see Teen Chef Tip)

1 tsp dried minced onion

½ tsp granulated garlic

1 tbsp (15 ml) soy sauce

Sliced green onion, for topping

Combine the beef stock, ramen cake, minced onion, granulated garlic and soy sauce in a small saucepan. Bring the mixture to a boil over medium-high heat. This should take about 5 minutes.

When the mixture comes to a boil, turn off the heat and cover the pot. Let the ramen sit, covered, on the hot stove, for 5 more minutes until the noodles are loose and tender.

Pour into a bowl and top with the green onion.

TEEN CHEF TIP: You can find ramen cakes other than the ubiquitous "instant ramen" varieties. We like the Halo brand ramen and find that the flavor is much better when we add our own spices and broth. If you want to try a gluten-free ramen cake, you may need to decrease the overall cook time. Just check the noodles after they have sat covered for a couple of minutes.

OVERLOADED POTATO WEDGES

SERVINGS: 1–2

No need to wait a long time for potatoes to bake or for fries to cook in the oven for this satisfying snack! These potato wedges are loaded with all the good stuff—bacon, cheese, ranch and green onions. Even better, they can be ready to enjoy in only about 15 minutes! Using the microwave or Instant Pot to partially cook the potatoes before finishing them in the oven significantly speeds up their cooking time. Using this method, it's easy to enjoy a plate of loaded potatoes for an awesome any-day snack.

2 small to medium russet potatoes

2 tbsp (28 g) unsalted butter, melted

¼ cup (28 g) crumbled cooked bacon

½ cup (56 g) shredded sharp Cheddar cheese

2 tbsp (30 ml) ranch dressing

2 green onion tops, sliced

Slice the potatoes into wedges and arrange them flat on a sturdy oven-safe plate. Cover the potatoes with a lightly damp paper towel and microwave them for 5 to 7 minutes until the potatoes are fork tender. Alternately, you can cook them in an Instant Pot for 5 minutes on a trivet with a cup of water underneath, transferring them to an oven-safe plate once they are softened.

Turn the oven on to the broil setting and let it heat for at least 5 minutes. Remove the plate of potatoes from the microwave and brush them with the melted butter. Immediately place the plate of potatoes under the broiler. Broil the buttered potatoes until they are crisp and browned.

Remove the potatoes from the oven and add the bacon and cheese. Return the plate to the oven and broil until the cheese is melted and bubbly.

Top the loaded potatoes with a drizzle of ranch dressing and the sliced green onion tops.

TEEN CHEF TIPS: Adding a damp paper towel to cover your food in the microwave can help your food to heat evenly and to not dry out. When using a paper towel in the microwave, though, avoid stacking the towels or using them in the microwave for more than a few minutes at a time so they do not dry out and become a fire hazard.

Homemade ranch is so easy to make and SO delicious! All you need for my favorite homemade ranch is plain Greek yogurt, mayonnaise and spices from the cabinet. That's it! You can find a full recipe on my website: thispilgrimlife.com.

NEXT-LEVEL GRILLED CHEESE SANDWICHES

You're not going to want to miss this over-the-top grilled cheese sandwich! As wonderful as a classic grilled cheese sandwich is—butter, melted cheese, toasted bread—this recipe takes the standard to another level. Imagine the difference between a Honda Civic (perfectly good) and a Ferrari (jaw-dropping wow factor) and transfer that feeling to this fancy grilled cheese. The tangy sourdough bread, salty pesto sauce and creamy Gruyère are absolutely buttery, pull-apart, cheesy perfection.

Spread the butter on the outside of each piece of bread and then season the outside with the kosher salt, fresh ground pepper and garlic powder. Spread pesto sauce on the inside of one of the pieces.

Heat a skillet over medium heat and add the olive oil. When the skillet is warm and the oil is beginning to sizzle, place both pieces of bread butter side down in the skillet. Place the Gruyère and Cheddar cheese slices on the piece of bread with the pesto sauce.

When the cheese begins to look softer at the edges and the bread is beginning to brown on the pan, flip the empty piece of bread onto the stack of cheeses, then flip the sandwich over on the pan to finish cooking.

Remove the sandwich when the outside is toasted to your liking and the cheese is melted.

Slice and serve.

TEEN CHEF TIP: Pesto sauce is amazingly versatile, besides being amazingly delicious. It works wonderfully here in this grilled cheese, but it's also great as a pizza sauce, pasta sauce, topping for scrambled eggs, as a spread on toast and so on. The main ingredients in pesto are greens, garlic, Parmesan, olive oil and pine nuts. In the summertime, you can make a quick batch with fresh basil leaves and in the winter, pesto is easily made with a mix of winter greens like spinach, Swiss chard and kale.

MAKES: 1 SANDWICH

1 tbsp (14 g) unsalted butter

2 slices sourdough boule

¼ tsp kosher salt

¼ tsp fresh ground pepper

½ tsp garlic powder

2 tbsp (30 g) pesto sauce

1 tbsp (15 ml) olive oil

2 slices Gruyère cheese

1 slice sharp Cheddar cheese

CHOCOLATE CHIP MUFFINS WITH A TWIST

MAKES: 12 MUFFINS

⅓ cup (168 g) applesauce

⅓ cup (80 ml) honey

2 eggs

1 tsp vanilla

2½ cups (225 g) rolled oats

1½ tsp (7 g) baking powder

1 tsp baking soda

½ tsp sea salt

1 tsp orange zest

¾ cup (126 g) mini chocolate chips

Have you ever tried orange and chocolate together? The two flavors actually go really well together in baking. Give the combination a try with these super easy muffins where the batter is made completely with a blender! The recipe uses healthy ingredients like applesauce, honey, eggs and oats, making them a great afternoon snack that will fill you up and provide energy without a sugar crash. Because cleaning a muffin pan is one of my least favorite things ever, I suggest using parchment muffin liners for really easy cleanup!

Preheat the oven to 375°F (191°C). Grease a standard muffin pan.

Add the wet ingredients—applesauce, honey, eggs and vanilla—to a blender. Then add in the dry ingredients—oats, baking powder, baking soda and sea salt.

Turn the blender on and blend the muffin batter on medium speed until the mixture is uniform and smooth.

Turn off the blender and stir in the orange zest and chocolate chips.

Divide the muffin batter evenly in the prepared pan.

Bake for 18 minutes, until the tops of the muffins spring back when gently pressed.

TEEN CHEF TIP: Adding zest from citrus fruits (such as oranges, lemons, limes and grapefruit) to a batter is a simple way to boost the flavor of your baked goods. A microplane is an easy and efficient way to remove the zest (it's also useful for grating Parmesan cheese to top finished dishes, or for making chocolate shavings to use on The Best Party Popcorn (page 133) or a Homemade Mocha Frappuccino (page 120). If you don't have a microplane, you can zest citrus fruits using the small holes on a box grater. Carefully slide the fruit across the holes until the top layer of the fruit is finely shredded. Be careful not to overdo it, though. Continuing to zest into the white of the fruit (the "pith") will result in a bitter flavor in your zest. Less is more here!

EVERYONE'S FAVORITE TUNA SALAD

SERVINGS: 2

This tuna salad is packed with flavor, thanks to the addition of the apples, pickles and raisins, making it a great way to win over any reluctant tuna eaters and propelling it to the top spot as everyone's favorite tuna salad! Easy to throw together, nutritious and satisfying, tuna salad is perfect for a quick lunch on the go or an afternoon snack. Enjoy it with your favorite crackers, right out of the bowl or even as a variation of the salad wraps (page 72)!

1 (7-oz [207-ml]) can tuna in water

¼ cup (31 g) diced apple

2 tbsp (30 g) minced pickles

2 tbsp (18 g) raisins

¼ cup (60 ml) mayonnaise

Drain the water from the can of tuna and empty the tuna into a small mixing bowl.

Dice the apples and chop the pickles until each are roughly the size of a raisin so that everything is uniform in size.

Add the apples, pickles, raisins and mayonnaise to the tuna. Stir until everything is well incorporated.

Serve with your favorite crackers.

TEEN CHEF TIP: The flavor of the mayonnaise can really affect the overall taste of recipes where it is a primary ingredient. Mayo can taste different according to the type of oil that is used or the different seasonings included. You may find that you enjoy mayo with a stronger tasting oil like olive oil or you prefer a more neutral oil like avocado or canola oil. Hellman's mayonnaise and Duke's mayonnaise are two great tasting, commonly found mayos. Primal Kitchen and Chosen Foods are two other brands with options for mayos with alternative, healthier oils. If you have no mayo on hand, but have a craving for tuna salad, you can make a simple homemade mayo with just a few eggs, lemon juice and oil (olive, avocado, canola) in a Mason jar with an immersion blender (find the recipe on my site: thispilgrimlife.com/homemade-mayonnaise).

RIDICULOUSLY GOOD HAM SLIDERS

**MAKES:
12 SANDWICHES**

You might be the most popular person in the house when these sliders come out of the oven and fill the air with their incredible aroma! That is, only if you plan on sharing. It's hard to go wrong with anything toasted in sweet rolls and this recipe is no exception. Ham and mozzarella cheese toasted with apple butter is a delicious, addictive sandwich combination! These sliders come together quickly and make an extra special afternoon snack. Go ahead and make extra because they freeze and reheat well.

12 Hawaiian dinner rolls

4 tbsp (56 g) butter, room temperature

½ tsp kosher salt

½ tsp fresh ground pepper

⅓ cup (103 g) apple butter

½ lb (226 g) sliced deli ham

2 cups (224 g) shredded mozzarella cheese

Turn the oven on, using the broil setting.

Slice the dinner rolls in half and lay them on a baking sheet, cut sides up. Spread butter over the rolls and then season with the kosher salt and fresh ground pepper. Place the dinner rolls in the oven under the broiler until they are lightly toasted, for 2 to 3 minutes.

Take the dinner rolls out of the oven. With the rolls still laying open, spread a small amount of apple butter on one side of each of the rolls. Top the rolls with 1 or 2 slices of ham and the shredded mozzarella cheese.

Return the baking sheet of sandwiches back to the oven under the broiler. Heat the sandwiches for 4 to 5 minutes, until the cheese is melted and the edges of the rolls are toasted.

Remove the baking sheet from the oven once again. Carefully close the sandwiches and serve.

TEEN CHEF TIP: You can make a batch of these and freeze some of them for later! Let the sandwiches cool completely before transferring them to a freezer bag. Remove as much of the air as you can, then freeze. To reheat, wrap a sandwich in a small piece of foil and warm in a 350°F (177°C) oven for 15 minutes. Alternately, wrap a sandwich in a slightly damp paper towel and microwave 3 to 4 minutes until they are warm.

AWESOME BLACK BEAN TAQUITOS

The next time you're craving all your favorite Tex-Mex dips and toppings, but want something that will keep you full longer than chips and salsa, make a batch of these delicious taquitos! The filling ingredients are super easy to keep on hand, and the mixture comes together quickly so you're not left waiting on snack time for very long. Serve them with salsa, guacamole and/or Greek yogurt for dipping, plus some tortilla chips on the side to scoop up anything that falls out!

Preheat the oven to 400°F (204°C). Lightly grease a baking sheet.

In a small mixing bowl, stir together the black beans, green chiles, Greek yogurt, Cheddar cheese, kosher salt, chili powder, granulated garlic and ground cumin.

Add a ⅓ cup–sized (80 ml) helping of the filling mixture to a tortilla and roll it into a tight log. Place it on a baking sheet, seam side down. Repeat until you've filled all the tortillas. Spray the tops of the tortillas with olive oil or brush them with olive oil if you don't have spray.

Bake in the preheated oven for 10 to 12 minutes, until the tortillas are crisp and browning at the edges.

Serve with salsa, sour cream/plain yogurt and/or guacamole for dipping.

To freeze for later, place cooled taquitos in a freezer bag and freeze. To reheat, place frozen taquitos in a 350°F (177°C) oven on a baking sheet for 15 minutes. Alternately, microwave for 3 to 5 minutes until the center is hot.

TEEN CHEF TIP: Corn tortillas have a great flavor but are more difficult to roll and fold without them cracking. Save the corn tortillas for enchiladas and tacos. Flour tortillas are easier to work with when making taquitos and freeze well too.

1 (15-oz [444-ml]) can black beans, rinsed and drained

1 (4-oz [118-ml]) can green chiles

¼ cup (60 ml) Greek yogurt

1½ cups (170 g) shredded Cheddar cheese

½ tsp kosher salt

½ tsp chili powder

½ tsp granulated garlic

½ tsp ground cumin

8 (8-inch [20-cm]) flour tortillas

OPTIONAL ADDITIONS
Salsa

Sour cream or plain yogurt

Guacamole

Tortilla chips

TAKE-ANYWHERE ENERGY BITES

MAKES: 12 BALLS

Keep these energy balls stashed in the refrigerator for a convenient snack when you're hungry. You can satisfy a craving for something sweet and give your body a quick protein boost at the same time! They are easy to make, easy to eat and much less expensive than their store-bought alternative. Energy balls are often made with chocolate morsels, but using dried fruit keeps them more portable and less messy.

1½ cups (278 g) oats

½ cup (129 g) peanut butter

⅓ cup (80 ml) honey

⅓ cup (48 g) dried fruit (raisins, dried cranberries and dried blueberries are favorites)

¼ cup (34 g) lightly salted sunflower seeds

1 tbsp (10 g) chia seeds

½ tsp almond extract

Combine the oats, peanut butter, honey, dried fruit, sunflower seeds, chia seeds and almond extract in a medium-sized mixing bowl. Stir the mixture together until everything is well incorporated and the oats are all coated with the wet ingredients. Place the bowl in the fridge and refrigerate for at least 30 minutes (the mixture will be easier to form into balls when it is chilled).

Spoon out heaping tablespoon-sized (15 ml) portions of dough and roll them into tight 1-inch (2.5-cm) balls. Keep the balls in the refrigerator until you're ready to eat them.

TEEN CHEF TIP: Chia seeds can act as a great binder in many recipes because they absorb liquid and create a gel-like consistency. They're often used to make quick puddings and jams, overnight oatmeal (page 116) or as a substitute for egg in baking recipes (mix 1 tablespoon [10 g] of chia seeds with 3 tablespoons [45 ml] of water and let it sit for 10 minutes before using). High in fiber, omega-3s and antioxidants, they're great to keep on hand in your kitchen!

I'LL TAKE MY BREAKFAST TO GO

If teenagers have a reputation for eating a lot, the flip side is sleeping a lot. However, just like teenagers' need for extra food, all the extra sleep is necessary and important too.

Which is exactly why I have included this chapter for breakfast recipes that can be made ahead of time and taken to go in the morning. A little bit of time in the week to stock your fridge and freezer means you can sleep in longer and still have a delicious and filling breakfast every day.

I'm admittedly not always the best at getting up in the morning and getting out the door on time can be a struggle. But I also know that skipping breakfast is not the healthiest way to start the day. Eating nutrient-dense foods like eggs, whole grains and fruit first thing helps to improve your mood, focus, energy levels, overall health and even helps promote healthy body weight.

I am always thankful to have breakfast foods like the Best Ever Breakfast Sandwiches (page 107) or Stuffed French Toast (page 108) in the freezer, or Healthy Egg Bites (page 115) or Super Easy Grab-&-Go Overnight Oatmeal (page 116) in the refrigerator. There's even a recipe for an amazing Homemade Mocha Frappuccino (page 120) that can save you a trip to the coffee shop, saving you both time and money!

BEST EVER BREAKFAST SANDWICHES

MAKES: 12 HALVED CROISSANTS

You know what's even better than eating a buttery croissant for breakfast? That same croissant, but filled with savory sausage, tender scrambled eggs and melted cheese! You can skip the breakfast drive-thru (saving time and money) if you set aside about half an hour and prep a batch of these croissant sandwiches for the freezer. Simply heat one up in the morning before you head out the door and enjoy a delicious, handheld breakfast on the go!

8 eggs

½ cup (120 ml) whole milk

½ tsp kosher salt

1 lb (226 g) uncooked ground breakfast sausage

1 cup (113 g) shredded Cheddar cheese

6 large croissants, sliced in half widthwise

3 tbsp (42 g) unsalted butter, room temperature

In a medium-sized mixing bowl, beat the eggs, whole milk and kosher salt together with a fork just until the mixture is uniform. Set aside.

Heat a large skillet over medium heat. Brown the breakfast sausage in the skillet, stirring and cooking for 5 to 6 minutes until the meat is no longer pink. Drain any excess grease (see the Teen Chef Tip on page 39). Turn the heat down to medium-low and then pour in the egg mixture and let the eggs cook for 3 to 4 minutes before stirring and scrambling them with the crumbled sausage.

When the eggs are completely cooked, turn off the heat. Spread the egg and sausage mixture into a flat layer in the pan. Evenly sprinkle the shredded cheese across the eggs.

Cut the croissant halves open and spread butter inside the croissants. Cut the sausage, egg and cheese filling into 12 portions. Try not to mix it up after you add the cheese so that the filling will stay together better. Add a portion of the filling to each croissant half. Fold the croissant sandwich closed, gently pressing the top of the sandwich onto the warm melted cheese.

To save for later, wrap each breakfast sandwich in a small square of foil (if planning to reheat in the oven), or in a paper towel (if planning to reheat in the microwave). Transfer the breakfast sandwiches to a freezer bag and freeze.

To reheat, warm the sandwiches in a 350°F (177°C) oven for approximately 20 minutes, or microwave them for 3 to 4 minutes. Do not remove foil for the oven or the paper towel for the microwave.

TEEN CHEF TIP: The key to keeping these croissants together and preventing the filling from falling out is the cheese. The cheese melted across the top acts as a glue, and if you add the filling to the croissants while the cheese is still warm, it will help to keep the croissants sealed too.

STUFFED FRENCH TOAST

Satisfy your sweet tooth and still have a protein-rich breakfast with these fun French toast sandwiches! This on-the-go breakfast is a delicious pairing of sweet jam, tangy cream cheese and crisp French toast. Like many of the breakfasts in this chapter, they can be made ahead of time, so making breakfast is one less thing to worry about in your already busy morning. Try different combinations of jam and cream cheese flavors to keep things interesting!

4 eggs

¼ cup (60 ml) whole milk

½ tsp cinnamon

2 tbsp (28 g) butter, divided

8 slices of sandwich bread

4 oz (112 g) cream cheese, room temperature

¼ cup (60 g) jam

Mix together the eggs, whole milk and cinnamon in a baking dish.

Heat a skillet over medium heat. Melt a ½ tablespoon (7 g) of butter in the pan and then submerge two bread slices in the egg mixture. Keep the slices in the egg mixture for about 1 minute per side, before removing them and letting the excess egg drip off the bread. Fry the eggy bread slices on both sides until they are toasted, about 3 minutes per side.

As they finish, set the French toast on a plate to cool. Repeat submerging in the egg mixture and frying, adding a ½ tablespoon (7 g) of butter to the pan each time, until you have 8 slices of French toast.

Spread the cream cheese on four of the slices of French toast, and jam on the other four. Press the slices together to make four sandwiches, each sandwich having a cream cheese and a jam side.

To freeze for later, wrap each sandwich in a piece of foil and place in a freezer bag. Heat in the oven on 350°F (177°C) for 15 to 20 minutes. Alternately, skip the foil, freeze in a freezer bag and reheat each sandwich in the microwave wrapped in a slightly damp paper towel for 3 to 4 minutes.

TEEN CHEF TIPS: French toast is best with thick slices of bread that are staler, or dried out, rather than with fresh and soft (making it an excellent way to use up the last of a loaf of bread). When selecting bread for this recipe, try to choose thicker sliced bread. If you are working with fresh bread, you can help dry it out by spreading it in a flat layer on a baking sheet and putting it in a 200°F (93°C) oven for about 20 minutes (flip the bread after 10 minutes). Now your bread is ready to absorb just the right amount of egg without yielding soggy pieces of French toast!

Making your own jam from scratch does not have to be complicated or require large quantities of fruit or canning. My favorite go-to jam for sandwiches, toast, toaster pastries and more is made from only 3 ingredients—berries, honey and chia seeds. You can use a variety of berries, add honey to taste and then use chia seeds to help the fruit mixture to gel or "jam up." The whole process takes less than 30 minutes! You can find the full recipe on my website: thispilgrimlife.com.

PEANUT BUTTER & CHOCOLATE PROTEIN SMOOTHIE

¾ cup (180 ml) whole milk

2 tbsp (30 ml) honey, local if possible

½ cup (120 ml) plain Greek yogurt

¼ cup (65 g) creamy peanut butter

1 tbsp (5 g) cocoa powder

½ cup (120 g) frozen avocado

½ cup (120 g) ice

Start your morning off with the energy and strength you need to make it to lunch with this protein-packed peanut butter smoothie! You can quickly mix everything together in a blender and transfer it to a portable cup for a healthy breakfast on the go. If you've never added avocado to a smoothie before, give it a try here. The avocado adds extra creaminess (and extra nutrition). You can find frozen avocado ready to go in the freezer section of many grocery stores.

Add the whole milk, honey and Greek yogurt to the blender first and then top with the remaining ingredients—peanut butter, cocoa powder, frozen avocado and ice.

Blend the smoothie on high until the mixture is smooth and the ingredients are fully incorporated. Add more milk, a couple tablespoons (30 ml) at a time, to adjust the consistency to your preference.

Serve or refrigerate immediately.

TEEN CHEF TIP: Protein is an essential part of a healthy diet. Starting your day with a good source of protein can help you stay full longer and provide the energy you need. Peanut butter, yogurt and milk are all beneficial sources of protein. Using avocado in this recipe adds in even more protein, as well as being a great source of healthy fats and fiber.

BETTER-THAN-BOXED TOASTER PASTRIES

MAKES: 8 PASTRIES

1 (8-oz [224-g]) portion of pie dough

2–3 tbsp (16–24 g) all-purpose flour

¾ cup (180 g) jam

1 egg

Chef beware! These toaster pastries should come with a warning label. After you eat the homemade version, you'll have a very hard time going back to the boxed variety. That's okay, though, because they're quite simple to make, especially if you use jam as a ready-to-go filling. Make a batch to share with your family right away or freeze the pastries to heat for a delicious morning treat.

Preheat the oven to 425°F (218°C). Remove your pie dough from the refrigerator about 15 minutes before you're ready to roll it out.

Lightly dust your work surface with flour. Roll the pie dough out into a large rectangle. If your rolling pin sticks to the dough, you can lightly dust the top with flour as well. Use a ruler to measure and cut ten 3 x 5-inch (8 x 20-cm) rectangles in your pie dough.

Dollop half of the rectangles with 2 tablespoons (30 g) of jam each, leaving a ½-inch (1.3-cm) border around all the sides. Top the jammed rectangles with the remaining rectangles. Use a fork to seal the edges, pressing around all four sides from the top and into the bottom layer. Use the fork to poke a few holes in the top of the pastries to allow steam to release.

Gather any pie dough scraps to press together and roll out again. Repeat rolling, cutting and filling until you've used all your pie dough.

Lay the pastries on a parchment-lined or greased baking sheet, about 1 inch (2.5 cm) apart. Beat the egg in a small bowl and then brush the beaten egg on the top of each of the pastries.

Bake in the preheated oven for 12 to 14 minutes, until the tops are golden brown.

To freeze for later, let the pastries cool completely, and then transfer them to a large zipper freezer bag. Freeze in a flat, single layer. When you're ready to reheat the pastries, do so in a 400°F (204°C) oven until they are hot.

TEEN CHEF TIP

HOW TO MAKE A SUGAR GLAZE: Mix together ¾ cup (90 g) powdered sugar with 1 tablespoon (15 ml) of water until you get a thick icing. It will seem like there's not enough water at first but keep stirring. If you do need to add additional water, add only a drop or two at a time because it thins out quickly. This thick glaze is great for drizzling on these toaster pastries or on other baked goods to create a white, stand-out drizzle.

HEALTHY EGG BITES

MAKES:
12 MINI FRITTATAS

When you need a breakfast that's the perfect blend of convenience and ease with taste and healthiness, turn to these mini frittatas! They're your favorite omelets, just handheld and portable. Plus, they're so easy to make—just mix the ingredients together in a bowl and bake in a muffin pan! Store them in the fridge for 3 to 4 days for a quick breakfast or snack.

12 eggs

½ cup (120 ml) heavy cream

½ cup (66 g) crumbled bacon

½ cup (15 g) chopped spinach

⅓ cup (50 g) cheese (feta or Cheddar)

½ tsp kosher salt

Preheat the oven to 350°F (177°C).

Stir the eggs together with a fork in a medium-sized mixing bowl until they are scrambled and the whites and yellows are well-blended. Add the heavy cream, crumbled bacon, chopped spinach, cheese and kosher salt, and stir.

Line a muffin pan with parchment paper muffin cups or grease the cups with an oil spray. Pour the egg mixture evenly into the muffin cups.

Bake for 20 minutes, or until the tops of the frittatas spring back when gently pressed.

Remove the frittatas from the oven and let them cool 5 minutes before removing them from the muffin pan. Eat immediately or refrigerate them for up to 5 days once cooled.

TEEN CHEF TIP: These mini frittatas never get boring because there are so many variations and ways to change them up! Try a pizza style frittata with mozzarella cheese and roasted tomatoes, a savory frittata with sausage and sautéed mushrooms or a veggie frittata with broccoli, spinach and caramelized onions. When you do try new ways to make a recipe, jot down what you did in the margin of the cookbook, or use a sticky note, so you will remember for next time!

SUPER EASY GRAB-&-GO OVERNIGHT OATMEAL

½ cup (92 g) old-fashioned oats

⅓ cup (80 ml) whole milk

¼ cup (60 ml) plain Greek yogurt

1 tbsp (10 g) chia seeds

2 tsp (9 g) brown sugar

½ tsp ground cinnamon

¼ cup (37 g) blueberries

Move over breakfast cereal, overnight oats are where it's at! This jar of goodness is simultaneously refreshing, delicious and good for you. And making them is as easy as stirring together a handful of ingredients before bed. You can enjoy them simply as is, top them with fresh or frozen fruit or have some fun and add whatever nuts, seeds, jam or granola that sound appealing. In a hurry in the morning? Not a problem. Grab your jar of oats from the fridge and you're set!

Combine the old-fashioned oats, whole milk, Greek yogurt, chia seeds, brown sugar and ground cinnamon in a pint-sized (473 ml) Mason jar. Stir well until everything is incorporated.

Refrigerate overnight, or at least 5 hours.

In the morning, give the oat mixture a stir and top with the blueberries. Stir in 1 or 2 tablespoons (15 to 30 ml) of additional milk to thin the mixture if it is too thick for your preference. Enjoy cold, or heat in the microwave about 1 minute until it is warm, mixing again to prevent any hot spots.

TEEN CHEF TIP

DIFFERENT KINDS OF OATMEAL: Oats are processed in different ways, resulting in the various types of oatmeal you'll find in the store. Steel cut oats are the coarsest and require the longest cooking time. They have the heartiest, chewiest texture. Old-fashioned or rolled oats are more processed and are great for baking and in this case, for overnight oats. They hold their texture well, while still softening and becoming tender. Instant or quick cook oats are thinner and smaller than old-fashioned and have the fastest cook time. They are not ideal for overnight oats because after soaking all night, they would be mush in the morning.

KILLER BREAKFAST BURRITOS

Enjoy your favorite Mexican flavors and start the day with a handheld fiesta for breakfast! You can have all the fresh, bold flavors with the simplicity of a burrito you can carry with you. Mix your favorite jarred salsa with cheesy scrambled eggs and then add any other favorite taco additions like hot sauce, corn salsa, jalapeños, etc. Roll the mixture in large tortillas and keep your burritos ready to go whenever you want a breakfast that is anything but boring!

8 eggs

½ cup (120 ml) whole milk

½ tsp kosher salt

1 tbsp (14 g) butter

¼ cup (28 g) green peppers, diced (optional)

¼ cup (40 g) onion, diced (optional)

1 cup (113 g) shredded Cheddar cheese

½ cup (132 g) salsa

4 large flour tortillas

In a medium-sized mixing bowl, stir together the eggs, whole milk and kosher salt with a fork. Heat a skillet over medium-low heat, and add the butter to the pan. When the butter starts to sizzle, pour in the egg mixture. Let the eggs cook for a couple of minutes without stirring and then use a spatula to scramble the eggs while they finish cooking.

If you'd like to have green pepper and onion in your egg burrito, sauté them in a separate small pan until they are browned and tender.

Transfer the cooked scrambled eggs to a mixing bowl. Add the cheese, salsa and if using, sautéed onion and peppers. Mix well.

Divide the egg mixture between the four tortillas. To make a burrito, fold in the sides of a tortilla. Then, while holding the sides in place, tightly roll to make a burrito. Repeat for all the tortillas. Enjoy right away or wrap each burrito in foil and freeze to save for later.

To reheat, place the foil-wrapped burrito in a 350° (177°C) oven for 30 minutes. Alternately, heat a burrito without the foil in the microwave for 4 to 5 minutes.

TEEN CHEF TIP: The key to fluffy scrambled eggs is mixing together your eggs and milk well with a fork, then cooking over medium-low heat and stirring often once they begin to set. Remove the pan from the heat just before you think they are done because the eggs will finish cooking in the pan, but leaving them on the heat too long will result in dry, over-cooked eggs.

HOMEMADE MOCHA FRAPPUCCINO

This homemade Frappuccino is sunshine and happiness in a glass! Coffee, chocolate and cream—yes, please! It's a delightfully refreshing drink that you can make at home with just a blender and a handful of basic ingredients. Enjoy one in the morning as a fun mid-morning boost or in the afternoon for a fun treat—just be sure to remember to use decaf coffee if it's late in the day!

½ cup (120 ml) milk

2 cups (480 g) ice

¼ cup (60 ml) maple syrup

2 tbsp (15 g) cocoa powder

1 cup (240 ml) coffee (cold or room temperature)

MAPLE WHIPPED CREAM
¼ cup (80 ml) heavy cream

1 tsp maple syrup

OPTIONAL TOPPING
Chocolate bar

To make the Frappuccino, combine the milk, ice, maple syrup, cocoa powder and coffee in a blender. Blend until the mixture is completely smooth. Pour it into a large glass.

Make the maple whipped cream with a milk frother, or by combining the heavy cream and maple syrup in a clean blender, then blending on a medium low speed for 2 to 3 minutes, until the cream becomes stiff in the blender.

Top the Frappuccino with the maple whipped cream. If you want something extra special, you can use a microplane or grater and a piece of chocolate to add shaved chocolate on top.

TEEN CHEF TIP: There are many ways to make whipped cream at home from scratch, but the first essential step is to start with cold heavy cream. Add a little syrup, maybe a little vanilla and then blend it until soft peaks form, either with a stand mixer, in a blender or with a milk frother. Just be careful you don't overmix it and end up with butter when the fat and liquid separate!

EPIC FOOD FOR PARTIES & GATHERINGS

Hosting friends and cooking for others is something I fell in love with in college and have been doing ever since. In that time, I've learned two valuable lessons. First, there is great power in taking the initiative, creating the opportunities and not waiting for a perfect time or space (spoiler—perfection doesn't exist, but imperfect hospitality is even better). If you want to get to know someone, hang out with your friends, mark a special day with people you care about and so on, you can be the one to make it happen.

Second, when it comes to planning food for parties and gatherings, simple is almost always better, and food that can be easily finished before your first guests arrive is best. Keep it simple and reserve your energy. Likewise, do what you can (including cutting corners and taking shortcuts) to be mostly finished and ready to focus on your people.

All the recipes in this chapter keep those two lessons in mind. The recipes are fun and perfect for parties and gatherings. They're also easy to prep ahead and then to set out and let friends help themselves.

Set out a Crazy Delicious Hot Dog Bar (page 129) your friends won't soon forget, take fajita packets to the bonfire (page 134), or keep the meal extra easy with a big pan of Totally Loaded Nachos (page 126). If you're more in need of delicious, shareable appetizers, check out the Homemade Potato Chip Dip (page 130) or the Comeback Snack Mix (page 138). The party popcorn (page 133), white chocolate bark (page 125) and decadent hot chocolate (page 137) will satisfy anyone's sweet tooth!

SWEET & SALTY WHITE CHOCOLATE BARK

SERVINGS: 6–8

1 (11-oz [308-g]) bag white chocolate chips

1 (5.2-oz [146-g]) can regular potato chips

OPTIONAL ADD-INS
½ cup (56 g) chopped pretzels, sliced almonds or peanuts

Would you like a jaw-dropping dessert idea? Better yet, a dessert that shocks people with how good it is, AND is also ridiculously easy?! This Sweet & Salty White Chocolate Bark is just the thing. The contrast of salty potato chips with the sweet, melted chocolate is perfection and, as the mixture cools, it forms a "bark" that you can break into bite-sized pieces.

You can use any plain potato chip for this recipe, but my favorite way to make this is with the chips that come in the tall can. They keep their crunch and shape well, even after being mixing together with the melted chocolate. Make the bark plain or try different add-ins (pretzels are an amazing addition!).

Melt 1 cup (240 g) of white chocolate chips over low heat in a heat-safe bowl. Alternately, you can melt them in microwave.

Add 1 cup (34 g) of roughly crushed potato chips to a mixing bowl. Stir in the pretzels, almonds or peanuts if you are using them. Pour in the melted chocolate and stir until all the chips are lightly coated with chocolate.

Transfer the chip mixture to a piece of parchment paper and press into a flat layer with a rubber spatula. Let the mixture cool completely. The bark will harden once it is cooled and you can then break it up into chucks.

TEEN CHEF TIP: Use low, gradual heat and a heavy-bottomed ramekin or pot when melting chocolate on the stove. Once the chocolate begins to have a sheen, it is almost ready to start melting, and once about half of the chocolate is soft and melted, you can remove the chocolate from the heat and stir until it is smooth. Scorching chocolate is no fun, so pay attention because the melting process doesn't take long!

TOTALLY LOADED NACHOS

Check out this recipe if you want to feed a big group of friends without breaking the bank or spending a lot of time in the kitchen! A large tray of nachos is an awesome way to serve a group because nachos are easily customizable according to everyone's preferences. Make the nachos ready to go with toppings already added, or make the base and set out toppings so your friends can assemble their own plates.

Given how easy, cheap and tasty sheet pan nachos are, you'll be wanting to have them a lot more than just on party days!

8 cups (256 g) of tortilla chips

1 (14.5-oz [429-ml]) can pinto beans, drained and rinsed

3 cups (339 g) shredded Mexican blend or Cheddar cheese

½ cup (132 g) salsa

½ cup (120 ml) plain Greek yogurt

½ cup (120 g) guacamole

OPTIONAL ADDITIONAL TOPPINGS

Chopped jalapeño

Pickled red onions

Corn salsa

Avocado slices

Heat your oven using the broil setting.

On a sheet pan, spread the chips on a large baking sheet in a flat layer. Evenly distribute the pinto beans, then the shredded cheese. Place the sheet pan under the hot broiler for 5 to 7 minutes, until the cheese is melted and bubbly and the edges of the chips are toasted.

Add the salsa to the nachos. Drizzle on the Greek yogurt and then add dollops of guacamole. Serve the nachos with additional optional toppings on the side.

TEEN CHEF TIP: Greek yogurt and sour cream can often be used interchangeably in recipes and as a topping in Mexican dishes. Greek yogurt is thick and tangy like sour cream and can be a healthier option than sour cream. I also simply find it easier to keep plenty of yogurt on hand, than trying to remember to keep both stocked.

CRAZY DELICIOUS HOT DOG BAR

SERVINGS: 6-8

Listen up, because this is going to be a new favorite way to feed your friends at parties! Everyone will be blown away with how delicious the toppings are with the hot dogs, even those who are skeptical at first about putting street corn on a hot dog. Just be ready to take the blame if no one is satisfied with plain hot dogs after trying this DIY hot dog bar!

You can find three tasty combination ideas in the recipe to try first—a homemade Sriracha coleslaw with pickled jalapeños, pimento cheese with pickled red onion and bacon, and Mexican Street Corn Made Easy (page 71) with guacamole. Each topping can be made ahead of time, or can be purchased ready to go, keeping your party preparations simple and easy.

Bring the water, red wine vinegar, ground cumin and ground nutmeg to a boil in a large stock pot. Carefully add the hot dogs, cover the pot and simmer for at least 10 minutes.

To make the Sriracha coleslaw, in a small mixing bowl, stir together the coleslaw mix, mayo and Sriracha until the coleslaw is evenly coated. Refrigerate the coleslaw until you're ready to serve the hot dogs.

Set up the DIY hot dog bar: Use small bowls to set out the toppings, putting the pairings next to each other as follows: (1) Sriracha coleslaw and pickled jalapeños, (2) pimento cheese with pickled red onion and bacon, and (3) Mexican Street Corn with guacamole (though of course there are no rules for assembling your hot dog). Don't forget to include serving utensils for each bowl.

Lay the hot dog buns open and flat on a large baking sheet. Brush them with a small amount of butter and then toast them in the oven until the insides are golden brown.

8 cups (1.9 L) water

2 tbsp (30 ml) red wine vinegar

⅛ tsp ground cumin

⅛ tsp ground nutmeg

2 8-packs beef hot dogs

SRIRACHA COLESLAW
3 cups (600 g) coleslaw mix

½ cup (120 ml) mayo

2 tbsp (30 ml) Sriracha

TOPPINGS
1 cup (240 g) pickled jalapeños

1 cup (224 g) pimento cheese

1 cup (240 g) pickled red onion

1 cup (112 g) bacon crumbles

Mexican Street Corn Made Easy (page 71)

1 cup (240 g) guacamole

FOR SERVING
16 hot dog buns

4 tbsp (56 g) butter, melted

TEEN CHEF TIP: Toasting buns before assembling burgers, hot dogs, sandwiches, etc. is a simple way to make a big difference in the tastiness of your final dishes. Besides just toasting with butter, a pinch of salt, a little garlic powder or a pinch of dried herbs can really elevate your burger/dog/sandwich!

HOMEMADE POTATO CHIP DIP

SERVINGS: 6–8

1 cup (120 ml) mayonnaise

1 cup (240 ml) plain Greek yogurt

1½ tsp (8 ml) Dijon mustard

1 tsp onion powder

1 tsp garlic powder

1 tsp dill

½ tsp kosher salt

If you need an EASY appetizer to bring to a party or make for your own gathering, throwing together a quick homemade dip is one of the easiest options! No need to buy a dip from the store when you see how simple this potato chip dip is to prepare with basic ingredients. The mustard is a nice zesty addition, and an equal mixture of mayonnaise and thick yogurt is an A-plus combination for creamy dips and dressings. Save the leftover chip dip to enjoy with crisp vegetables the next day at lunch!

Combine the mayonnaise, Greek yogurt, Dijon mustard, onion powder, garlic powder, dill and kosher salt in a jar or bowl. Stir well until all the spices are completely incorporated, making sure that nothing is clumping at the bottom.

Chill for at least one hour before serving.

Serve with potato chips or fresh, crisp vegetables.

TEEN CHEF TIP: I don't always follow this rule myself, but giving dips, sauces, etc. time to chill and time for the flavors to better meld together is a good habit. Your final dish will have more intense flavors than if you skip the chill time completely before serving. As for this chip dip, it's also just a lot tastier cold!

THE BEST PARTY POPCORN

SERVINGS: 6–8

Have fun with this party popcorn that is anything but boring! Make your favorite microwave popcorn, or follow the steps to make a pot of popcorn right on the stove. The caramel sauce is so delicious and comes together quickly—did you know sugar melts and turns to liquid?! So cool. Stick with only caramel on your popcorn, or after drizzling on the caramel, add a pinch of coarse salt, grated chocolate, coconut flakes, sprinkles, etc. Save any extra caramel for Super Fun Banana Split Milkshakes (page 156), or for topping your Homemade Mocha Frappuccino (page 120).

1 tbsp (15 ml) coconut oil

1 cup (208 g) popcorn kernels

CARAMEL DRIZZLE
½ cup (100 g) granulated sugar

3 tbsp (42 g) unsalted butter

¼ cup (60 ml) heavy cream

OPTIONAL TOPPINGS
Kosher salt

Shredded coconut

Grated chocolate

Heat a large pot over medium heat. Add the coconut oil to the pot. When the oil is melted, add one popcorn kernel. When the kernel pops, add the rest of the popcorn kernels. Shake the pot so that the kernels are coated with the hot oil, and then give them another little shake to put them back in a flat layer. Cover the pot and wait until the kernels are popping, giving the pot a shake once or twice. Take the pot off the heat once the popping begins to slow down. Empty the popcorn onto a large baking sheet.

To make the caramel drizzle, add the sugar to a small pot and heat over medium heat. The sugar will melt and caramelize. Once the sugar begins to turn liquid, stir constantly. When it is completely melted, reduce the heat to medium-low and add the butter. Stir constantly while the butter melts and incorporates into the sugar. Slowly pour the heavy cream in, stirring constantly until the mixture is smooth and uniform. Remove the pot from the heat.

Either immediately drizzle the caramel sauce on the popcorn or transfer it to a glass jar to cool. The sauce will thicken as it cools.

After you drizzle the caramel on the popcorn, if you want something extra, you can sprinkle it with kosher salt, shredded coconut or grated chocolate.

TEEN CHEF TIP: Making popcorn on the stove can seem tricky at first, but once you figure out the right temperature setting on your stove and know what to listen for, it is a simple and extra delicious way to enjoy popcorn!

A FEW TIPS FOR MAKING THE BEST STOVETOP POPCORN:

1. Use a heavy-bottomed pot for even heat distribution.

2. Fresh popcorn will pop better (stale, old popcorn dries out and it's the water inside the kernel that is needed to make it pop).

3. Stick to medium heat and don't try to speed up the process by cranking up the heat (or you might end up with burnt-tasting popcorn).

FIREPIT CHICKEN FAJITAS

Give your friends an extra memorable experience making individual fajitas around a fire! You can prep the foil packets ahead of time so there's no kitchen work to do after your friends arrive. Build your fire, and once it's ready, set the foil packets to cook about half an hour on the hot coals. Bring your tortillas and toppings to the fire pit, and there's no reason to go back inside. Simply hang out around the fire and enjoy some really delicious fajitas!

Tear off four 12-inch (30-cm) squares of foil.

Slice the chicken thighs into strips. Combine the strips of chicken, sliced onion and peppers in a medium-sized mixing bowl. Add the kosher salt, chili powder, oregano, granulated garlic and ground cumin to the bowl and stir to evenly coat the fajita mixture.

Divide the seasoned mixture between the four foil pieces, dolloping the chicken and vegetables in the middle of the foil. Evenly divide the sliced tomato on top of each mound of chicken and vegetables. Fold over all four sides to create a sealed packet.

Build a small fire in a fire pit and let the wood burn down to create a cooking area with hot coals. Place the foil packets directly on the hot coals, creating a cradle for them to cook in. Cook the packets for 20 to 25 minutes, until the vegetables are tender and the chicken is cooked through (an internal temperature of 175°F [79°C]).

Carefully remove the packets from the fire pit. Serve the fajita mixture on flour tortillas, with your favorite toppings such as sour cream, shredded lettuce, shredded cheese, salsa, guacamole, etc.

1½ lb (681 g) boneless chicken thighs

1 cup (160 g) sliced yellow onion

2 sliced bell peppers

2 tsp (12 g) kosher salt

1 tbsp (5 g) chili powder

2 tsp (3 g) oregano

1 tsp granulated garlic

1 tsp ground cumin

1 sliced tomato

4-5 flour or corn tortillas, to serve

OPTIONAL TOPPINGS
Sour cream

Shredded lettuce

Shredded cheese

Salsa

Guacamole

TEEN CHEF TIP: Cooking over the fire requires a large bed of coals for even heat and even temperatures. The easiest campfire to build is the "log cabin" style in which the wood is stacked crisscross on top of each other. Be sure to use dry wood, as it will be easier to light and will produce less smoke. Once the fire has burned down to mostly a bed of coals, you are ready to add your packets to cook.

DECADENT HOT CHOCOLATE WITH SPRUCED UP MARSHMALLOWS

SERVINGS: 6–8

8 cups (1.9 L) whole milk

1 pint (480 ml) half and half

1 cup (224 g) dark chocolate morsels

½ cup (100 g) granulated sugar

½ cup (40 g) cocoa powder

1 tsp cinnamon

Pinch of kosher salt

You'll definitely want to share this decadent hot chocolate with friends because it's too rich and chocolatey to enjoy all on your own! Using both whole milk and half and half makes this hot chocolate extra creamy, and the mixture of cocoa powder, dark chocolate and cinnamon creates great flavor. Combine everything in a slow cooker, Instant Pot, or a large pot on the stove and keep it warm until you're ready to ladle it into mugs.

While the hot chocolate heats, dip jumbo marshmallows in simple syrup, and then roll in the fun toppings for an awesome bonus with huge appeal!

SPRUCED UP MARSHMALLOWS

¼ cup (50 g) granulated sugar

1 (10-oz [280-g]) bag jumbo marshmallows

1 cup (192 g) crushed peppermint, shaved chocolate or sprinkles

Combine the whole milk, half and half, dark chocolate morsels, granulated sugar, cocoa powder, cinnamon and kosher salt in a large pot, Instant Pot or slow cooker. Heat the milk mixture until it is hot to the touch, almost to a simmer, but not boiling. Stir the hot chocolate until the chocolate is melted and all the ingredients are thoroughly incorporated.

Turn the pot or slow cooker to low or the keep warm setting. Ladle the hot chocolate into mugs once you're ready to serve.

To make the marshmallows, stir together the sugar with ¼ cup (60 ml) of hot water in a small bowl until the sugar is completely dissolved in the water. Use a toothpick to dip the marshmallows one at a time in the sugar water, and then roll the sugary marshmallow in the peppermint, chocolate or sprinkles. Set on a piece of parchment to dry. Serve with the hot chocolate.

TEEN CHEF TIP: Simple syrup is equal parts water and sugar. It's easy to make and useful to have on hand for anything that would need a liquid sweetener—think lemonade, mocktails and tea or coffee drinks. You can easily make it by mixing together hot water and sugar until the sugar is dissolved, and then storing it in a jar in the refrigerator for up to a month. Try different colors of sugars for different tastes (brown sugar will create a more caramel flavor) or try different additions to create flavored simple syrup (vanilla bean, citrus peel, fresh herbs, whole spices, etc.).

COMEBACK SNACK MIX

Whip up a batch of this seasoned snack mix and have the ultimate munching appetizer you and your friends will want to keep coming back to! Thankfully, the recipe makes a lot, which is perfect since the snack mix is super hard to resist. Don't let the combination of pickle juice, ketchup, mustard and spices deter you—each component comes together to create an addictive seasoning. Remember this recipe for your next game night or chill gathering!

Preheat the oven to 250°F (121°C).

In your largest mixing bowl, combine the cereals, pretzels and nuts. Use your hands to mix everything together. Transfer the mixture to your largest rimmed baking sheet.

Mix together the melted butter with the pickle juice, ketchup, mustard and seasonings (kosher salt, granulated garlic, onion powder and paprika). Pour the butter mixture over the snack mix. Carefully toss the snack mix and stir it around the baking sheet until all the pieces are buttered and seasoned. Spread the snack mix into a flat layer.

Bake in the preheated oven for 1 hour, stirring three times (every 15 minutes).

Let the snack mix cool, and then transfer to a serving bowl or container for storage.

9 cups (360 g) cereal (plain Cheerios™, Chex™, shredded wheat squares)

3 cups (120 g) thin pretzel sticks

3 cups (438 g) nuts (peanuts, cashews, walnuts and pecans work well)

¾ cup (180 ml) unsalted butter, melted

2 tbsp (30 ml) pickle juice

1 tbsp (15 ml) ketchup

1 tbsp (15 ml) yellow mustard

2 tsp (12 g) kosher salt

1½ tsp (4 g) granulated garlic

1½ tsp (4 g) onion powder

1 tsp paprika

TEEN CHEF TIP: Excess air and moisture is the enemy of keeping food crisp and crunchy. This is why vacuum sealers are so handy for preserving and storing food. If you have extra cereal after making this recipe, you can save it for another party or gathering—no vacuum sealer needed. Transfer the cereal to a zipper storage bag and close the bag, pressing out as much air as you can and only leaving a small opening. Insert a straw into the opening, seal the bag up to the straw, then suck out the remaining air from the bag. Carefully pull out the straw and seal the bag. Voila! Vacuum sealed.

THIS CALLS FOR SOMETHING SPECIAL

There is something intrinsically celebratory about desserts and treats. We say "treat yourself" when we want to do something extra, something above and beyond, something to make life a little sweeter. And that's definitely the case with desserts. Completely necessary? No. Completely worth it? Oh yes.

The desserts in this chapter vary in prep time and flavors, so there's something for any occasion. Need a cake that will wow your friends? Try the Legendary Double Cookie Ice Cream Cake (page 143). Forgot about a birthday or need a fast dessert you can top with candles? Try the Last-Minute Confetti Cookie Cake (page 148). Want a special dessert to share with the family? Try the Easiest Apple Pie & Homemade Whipped Cream (page 144).

I am, however, of the mindset that desserts should not be reserved only for special occasions. I'm a big fan of simple desserts that can be thrown together for indulging any day of the week, and occasionally any time of the day. Life is short, after all. Cookies, brownies, milkshakes—they are all easy enough for regular days and only require a few basic ingredients.

LEGENDARY DOUBLE COOKIE ICE CREAM CAKE

If you want to truly impress your friends with a dessert that looks and tastes like it came from a local ice cream shop or bakery, this is your chance! Ice cream cake is a huge crowd pleaser. Layers of cookie dough cake, chocolate cookies, ice cream and whipped cream are spread in layers and frozen. Once the entire cake is complete, the slices of cake show of each distinct layer, giving it major WOW factor!

In a medium-sized mixing bowl, stir together the cookie dough ingredients—start with combining the sugars and melted butter, then add the flour, chocolate chips, vanilla extract and whole milk, and stir until no streaks of flour remain and you have a soft, cohesive dough.

Grease the bottom of a 9 x 11-inch (23 x 28-cm) baking dish. Press the cookie dough into the bottom of the dish, evenly spreading it out so that it covers the entire bottom surface. Cover and freeze it for 30 minutes (or more) before adding the next layer.

Remove the ice cream from the freezer 10 to 15 minutes before spreading it on the cookie dough layer so it will soften and be easier to spread. Take the baking dish out of the freezer and cover the chilled cookie dough with the ice cream. You should have a thick, even layer. Cover the dish again and return it to the freezer for an hour (or more).

When the ice cream layer is frozen, remove the baking dish from the freezer. Crush the chocolate sandwich cookies (an easy way to do this is to put them in a zipper bag and pound them with the back of a spoon or bottom of a measuring cup). Pour the crushed cookies evenly across the top of the ice cream layer.

Cover the crushed cookies with the whipped cream, dolloping it evenly around the dish to avoid shifting the cookies too much. (It isn't necessary to freeze the cookie layer first). Use a spatula to smooth out the whipped cream layer and then cover the baking dish and return it to the freezer.

After one more hour (or more), remove the baking dish from the freezer and drizzle the top of the ice cream cake with alternating lines of chocolate and caramel syrup. You can make a zigzag pattern, stripes, write a message or whatever you like for this part!

Cover the baking dish and return the ice cream cake to the freezer. It will keep for several days until you're ready to serve it.

Let the ice cream cake sit out of the freezer for about 10 minutes before slicing and serving.

COOKIE DOUGH

⅓ cup (66 g) granulated sugar

⅔ cup (132 g) brown sugar

¾ cup (180 ml) melted butter

1½ cups (188 g) heat-treated all-purpose flour (see Teen Chef Tip)

1 cup (168 g) chocolate chips

1 tsp vanilla extract

¼ cup (60 ml) whole milk

ICE CREAM CAKE

1 gal (3.8 L) vanilla ice cream

1 (20-oz [560-g]) box chocolate crème sandwich cookies

14 oz (414 ml) ready-made whipped cream (about 2 canisters)

Chocolate sauce

Caramel sauce

TEEN CHEF TIP: When making cookie dough that will be eaten raw, like in this recipe, it's important to heat-treat your flour to make it safe for raw consumption. You can do this in the oven or the microwave. To heat-treat in the oven, heat the oven to 350°F (177°C) and spread the flour out on a baking sheet. Bake the flour for about 10 minutes, stirring once halfway through. To heat-treat in the microwave, pour the flour into a heat-safe bowl and heat for 30 second intervals, stirring after each, for 4 minutes total. With either method, the key is to heat the flour to 160°F (77°C) to remove any potentially harmful bacteria. Cool the flour before continuing to the next step.

EASIEST APPLE PIE & HOMEMADE WHIPPED CREAM

1 (8-oz [226-g]) portion/roll of pie dough

5 apples

¼ cup + 1 tbsp (64 g) granulated sugar, divided

2 tbsp (30 ml) lemon juice

2 tbsp (15 g) all-purpose flour

1 tsp ground cinnamon

¼ tsp ground nutmeg

3 tbsp (42 g) butter

1 egg

SPICED WHIPPED CREAM

1½ cups (360 ml) heavy cream

3 tbsp (45 ml) maple syrup

½ tsp cinnamon

⅛ tsp nutmeg

Let me let you in on a little secret—you can make one of the most popular, classic desserts in half the time and with half the work! Also called a galette, this is a simpler, "rustic" way to make a pie. You won't need a pie dish for this recipe because a galette is baked on a baking sheet. You'll find that galettes are perfect to make as spontaneous treats to share with your family and for simple desserts to share with friends. This recipe features a traditional apple filling, but you can use this same method with different fruit fillings, or even with delicious seasonal vegetables for a fancy appetizer.

Take your pie dough out of the fridge 30 minutes before you are ready to roll it out. Preheat the oven to 400°F (204°C).

Peel, core and cut the apples into thin slices. Add the apples to a medium-sized mixing bowl. Stir in the ¼ cup (50 g) sugar, lemon juice, flour, ground cinnamon and ground nutmeg. Let the apple mixture rest for 10 minutes while you roll out the pie dough.

Dust your countertop lightly with flour. Using a rolling pin, press out the pie dough to form a 12-inch (30-cm) circle that is about ¼ inch (6 mm) thick. Add the apple mixture to the pie dough, leaving about a 2½-inch (6-cm) border around the outside. Fold the pie dough up onto the apples, overlapping as needed to form a rustic circle. Slice the butter into 6 thin pieces and lay them on the apples, tucking a few under the pie dough you just folded up.

Beat an egg in a small bowl to make an egg wash and then brush it on the pie dough, discarding any extra egg wash. Sprinkle the remaining tablespoon (15 g) of sugar on the pie dough.

Bake in the preheated oven for 15 to 18 minutes, until the pie dough is browned and the apples are tender.

To make the spiced whipped cream, combine the heavy cream, maple syrup, cinnamon and nutmeg in a blender and blend on medium low speed until the cream forms soft peaks and stops moving around the blender. Alternately, you can whip the cream using a stand mixer and the whisk attachment. Combine all the ingredients in the bowl and turn the mixer on high until the cream forms soft peaks.

TEEN CHEF TIP: Pie dough is one of my absolute favorite foods. It's buttery and flaky and rich and perfect. It's been years since I have bought ready-to-go pie dough from the store because it only takes a handful of ingredients and less than 15 minutes to make it myself at home. (Unsurprisingly, homemade pie dough tastes better too). I like to use a mixture of cold butter and coconut oil in pie dough, but you can also use all butter for an even richer crust. I have the full recipe and even more pie dough inspiration on my website: thispilgrimlife.com!

OOEY-GOOEY S'MORES COOKIES

MAKES:
2 DOZEN COOKIES

Roasting marshmallows and making s'mores by the fire is so fun! With these cookies, you can replicate the fun and flavor anytime the craving strikes—no bonfire needed. All the key ingredients are present—graham crackers and chocolate are in the cookie itself and on top are marshmallows toasted and browned under the broiler, which gives these cookies an authentic presentation. Have fun seeing who can come up with the longest marshmallow "pull" (as shown in the picture)!

½ cup (120 ml) unsalted butter, melted

¼ cup (55 g) brown sugar

¾ cup (150 g) granulated sugar

1 tsp vanilla extract

2 eggs

1¼ cups (156 g) all-purpose flour

1 tsp baking soda

1 cup (84 g) crumbled graham crackers

1 cup (168 g) dark chocolate chips

2 cups (100 g) mini marshmallows

Preheat the oven to 375°F (191°C).

In a medium-sized mixing bowl, whisk together the melted butter and both sugars until they are completely blended together. Stir in the vanilla extract and then whisk in the eggs until the mixture is shiny and smooth.

In a separate small mixing bowl, combine the flour, baking soda and graham cracker crumbs. Add the flour mixture to the sugar mixture and gently stir until no streaks of flour remain. Fold in the dark chocolate chips.

Use half the dough to dollop tablespoon-sized (15 ml) balls onto a baking sheet that has been greased or lined with parchment paper. Gently press down on the balls of dough to flatten slightly. Bake in the preheated oven for 11 minutes.

Repeat the previous step with the remaining cookie dough.

Turn the oven on to the broil setting. Top the cookies with mini marshmallows and place the baking sheet under the broiler until the marshmallows are toasted, for 3 to 5 minutes.

TEEN CHEF TIP: Did you know that granulated sugar and brown sugar have different effects and purposes in baking? They usually can't be used interchangeably, even though they're both sweet and crumbly. Regular granulated sugar is a more mild sugar to use in baking, taking a backseat to other ingredients' flavors. Generally, using more granulated sugar results in thinner, crispier cookies. Brown sugar on the other hand has the added moisture and flavor from the molasses. More brown sugar often results in chewier, moister cookies.

LAST-MINUTE CONFETTI COOKIE CAKE

SERVINGS: 8–10

¾ cup (180 ml) butter, melted

1½ cups (300 g) granulated sugar

2 eggs

1 tsp vanilla extract

¾ tsp baking soda

½ tsp sea salt

2½ cups (313 g) all-purpose flour

2.75-oz (77-g) container confetti sprinkles

Do you need a last-minute dessert to pull out for spontaneous celebrations, or for times when you haven't had a chance to prepare a more elaborate dessert? Me too. This cookie cake fits both occasions and looks so fun when finished, which is why it gets put to use so often! The dough is mixed together in one bowl, then spread flat on a large pizza pan. You can even double the recipe and bake it on a large sheet pan for when you need even more cake to go around!

Preheat the oven to 375°F (191°C).

In a medium-sized mixing bowl, stir together the melted butter and granulated sugar until it's a consistent, sandy texture. Add the eggs and vanilla extract and stir well until they are completely blended. Stir in the baking soda, sea salt and flour until no streaks of flour remain. Fold in the confetti sprinkles.

Grease a 12-inch (30-cm) pizza pan or rimmed baking sheet and press the cookie cake dough into the pan, spreading it not quite to the edges (leaving some room to spread).

Bake in the preheated oven for 15 minutes, until the edges of the cookie cake are just turning brown and the center is cooked through.

Let it stand 10 minutes before slicing.

TEEN CHEF TIP: How long you stir a cookie dough matters—it is possible to overmix your dough (resulting in dense, flat cookies), or under-mix your dough (leaving you with pockets of raw flour or uneven baking). A good rule of thumb is to stop stirring when there are no remaining streaks of flour and everything is uniform. That's your signal that your dough is done being mixed. If you have ingredients to add to your cookie dough, like chocolate chips or in this recipe, sprinkles, stop stirring your dough when it is almost uniform. It will finish mixing as you stir in your final ingredients.

IMPRESSIVE CHOCOLATE PUDDING PIE

Calling all chocolate lovers! This pudding pie packs a serious chocolate punch, plus a seriously delicious layer of rich whipped cream. It's not a dessert for the faint of heart. You'll feel like a legit baker making your own pudding from scratch (easier than you think!) and making a simple graham cracker crust (though you could easily swap a ready-to-go one from the store). The most important thing to note about this pie is that you must make it several hours before you need it so the pudding has time to set. Didn't give yourself enough time? The Last-Minute Confetti Cookie Cake has your back (page 148).

Preheat your oven to 325°F (163°C).

Place the graham crackers in a zipper bag and smash them until they are fine crumbs. (If you have a food processor, you can blend the graham crackers using that.) Transfer the graham cracker crumbs to a mixing bowl and add the granulated sugar and melted butter. Stir the mixture with a fork until it looks like uniform, coarse, wet sand. Press the graham cracker mixture into a 9-inch (23-cm) pie dish, gently pressing the mixture down across the bottom and partially up the sides of the dish.

Bake the crust in the preheated oven for 13 minutes. Allow it to cool completely before filling.

To make the pudding, combine the granulated sugar, cocoa powder, kosher salt, corn starch and milk in a medium pot. Whisk the ingredients until everything is evenly incorporated and bring the mixture to a simmer over medium heat.

When the pudding mixture begins to simmer, add 2 egg yolks to a small bowl. Slowly whisk in about 1 cup (240 ml) of the hot pudding mixture into the egg yolks. Once the egg yolks are blended, stir the egg mixture back into the pudding pot. This process is called "tempering" the egg.

Bring the pudding to a low boil and then turn the heat down to medium-low. Simmer for 3 to 4 minutes until the pudding is thick, whisking often. Remove the pudding from the heat and stir in the chocolate morsels until they are melted and incorporated.

Pour the chocolate pudding onto the graham cracker pie crust. Smooth into a flat layer. Refrigerate for 3 hours before topping with whipped cream.

To make the whipped cream topping, combine the heavy cream, powdered sugar and vanilla extract in a stand mixer with the whisk attachment, or use a hand-held blender and medium-sized mixing bowl. Beat the cream mixture on high for 5 to 6 minutes until stiff peaks form. Fold the whipped cream on top of the chilled chocolate pudding.

Refrigerate the pie for at least 1 more hour before serving. If you'd like, grate chocolate on top of the pie or top with chocolate sprinkles.

CRUST
12 graham crackers

2 tbsp (30 g) granulated sugar

½ cup (120 ml) unsalted butter, melted

CHOCOLATE PUDDING FILLING
⅓ cup (66 g) granulated sugar

⅓ cup (27 g) cocoa powder

Pinch of kosher salt

¼ cup + 1 tbsp (37 g) corn starch

2 cups (480 ml) whole milk

2 egg yolks, at room temperature

½ cup (112 g) dark chocolate morsels

WHIPPED CREAM
1½ cups (360 ml) heavy cream

¼ cup (30 g) powdered sugar

½ tsp vanilla extract

TEEN CHEF TIP: This pudding does not take long to make, but the timing of each step is important. Whenever I am making a dessert or dish that requires closer attention, I make sure that all my ingredients are ready to go and put away any distractions until I finish. This pudding may seem more complicated than what you are used to, but I know you can do it! Remember, a recipe is only completely new the first time you try it. After you make something more technical, you will learn from each step and feel more confident to make it again.

AMAZING MINI POUND CAKES

MAKES:
12 INDIVIDUAL CAKES

You know how every family has a special dessert that gets made at almost every holiday? Have something in mind for yours? Old fashioned pound cake is mine. My grandmother always made the most amazing pound cake when I was growing up.

This recipe for Amazing Mini Pound Cakes is my grandmother's special recipe, but instead of one large cake, we're going to bake it up into a dozen personal-sized cakes! You'll love these cakes for special occasions too, preferably served with a cup of coffee or a glass of milk. The buttery, sweet cake is so delicious, though the best part is definitely the craggy, flaky crust that forms on top!

¾ cup (170 g) unsalted butter, room temperature

4 oz (112 g) cream cheese, room temperature

1½ cups (300 g) granulated sugar, plus more for sprinkling on top

3 eggs, room temperature

½ tsp vanilla extract

½ tsp almond extract

1½ cups (180 g) cake flour

Pinch of salt

Preheat the oven to 325°F (163°C).

In the bowl of a stand mixer (or in a medium-sized mixing bowl with a handheld mixer), combine the butter, cream cheese and granulated sugar. Mix on medium speed until the mixture is light and fluffy.

Turn the mixer to medium-low. Add each egg, one at a time, until each is incorporated into the batter. Add both extracts and mix well.

Turn the mixer to low and slowly add the flour and the pinch of salt. Continue to mix on low until the batter is smooth and no streaks of flour remain.

Grease a muffin pan and lightly dust the muffin cups with flour. Divide the batter evenly between the muffin cups. Sprinkle each cake with ¼ teaspoon of sugar.

Bake the pound cakes in the preheated oven for 30 minutes, or until a toothpick inserted into the center of a cake comes out clean. Let the cakes cool at least 10 minutes in the pan before carefully removing them to finish cooling on a wire rack.

TEEN CHEF TIP: Cake flour is flour that has been sifted multiple times to create a lighter, airier flour. Not using cake flour in cake recipes that call for it can result in denser cakes that do not rise as well. If you don't have any cake flour, you can make your own by sifting the flour four to five times through a sifter or wire straining basket.

EPIC PB CUP BROWNIES

There's a reason peanut butter cups are one of the most popular candies. Chocolate and peanut butter go together even better than peanut butter and jelly. If they're one of your favorite combos too, then you're going to love these rich and chocolatey brownies that have a surprise center layer of sweet peanut butter filling—just like a fudgy peanut butter cup!

I love how straightforward it is to make brownies, but I don't always love how I want to eat the entire pan if it's left on the counter. Thankfully, you can enjoy brownies one night and then freeze leftovers as individual brownies for another time when you want a quick dessert with extra-minimal effort.

1 cup (200 g) granulated sugar

½ cup (40 g) cocoa powder

1 cup (125 g) all-purpose flour

½ tsp sea salt

¾ cup (180 ml) butter, melted

3 eggs

1 tsp vanilla extract

½ cup (112 g) semi-sweet chocolate morsels

PEANUT BUTTER FILLING

1 cup (258 g) peanut butter (creamy or chunky)

½ cup (60 g) powdered sugar

2 tbsp (30 ml) butter, melted

Preheat the oven to 350°F (177°C).

Stir together the granulated sugar, cocoa powder, flour and sea salt in a medium-sized mixing bowl until the dry ingredients are well incorporated. Add the butter, eggs and vanilla extract to the bowl. Mix well until the batter is smooth and uniform. Stir in the chocolate morsels.

To make the filling, combine the peanut butter, powdered sugar and butter in a small mixing bowl and stir until smooth.

Grease an 8 x 8-inch (20 x 20–cm) baking dish. Pour half the brownie batter into the baking dish and spread it smooth across the bottom. Dollop the peanut butter filling on top of the batter and gently spread until smooth. Top the peanut butter filling with the second half of the brownie batter—again, dolloping the batter in small portions so that it is easier to spread flat and form a top layer.

Bake in the preheated oven for 25 to 30 minutes, until a toothpick inserted in the center comes out clean.

Cool 10 minutes before slicing.

TEEN CHEF TIP

CHOOSING CHOCOLATE INGREDIENTS: Three common chocolates used in baking are cocoa powder, semi-sweet chocolate and dark chocolate. Cocoa powder is unsweetened and can give a rich chocolate taste, or even be added to savory dishes like chili (see page 54) to increase the richness. Semi-sweet chocolate is in between milk chocolate and dark chocolate in terms of chocolate flavor. It's good to use if you want a sweeter finished product. Dark chocolate is rated by percentages according to its cocoa powder content, typically ranging from 30 percent to 80 percent. The higher the percentage, the more intense the flavor and potentially bitter the chocolate. In baking recipes that call for dark chocolate, I like to use one with ratings around 60 percent cocoa.

SUPER FUN BANANA SPLIT MILKSHAKES

SERVINGS: 2

1 large ripe banana

¼ cup (37 g) lightly salted roasted peanuts

¼ cup (56 g) chocolate morsels

2 cups (272 g) vanilla ice cream

1 cup (240 ml) whole milk, or milk of your choice

3 tbsp (45 ml) caramel sauce

Ready-made whipped cream and maraschino cherries, for topping

Milkshakes are such a fun treat when you want something sweet, cool and refreshing. These Super Fun Banana Split Milkshakes are no ordinary milkshakes, though. The chunks of ripe bananas, swirls of caramel and bits of peanut and chocolate make this milkshake extra special. This recipe makes two servings, so find a friend to share your masterpiece with. Don't forget the whipped cream and cherries on top!

Slice the banana into ½-inch (1.3-cm) pieces. Measure out the peanuts and chocolate morsels.

Combine the ice cream and milk in a blender. Mix briefly on medium-high to incorporate the two. Add the banana pieces, peanuts and chocolate to the blender. Pulse the blender a few times to incorporate the additions into the milkshake. Don't overmix (see Teen Chef Tip).

Add the caramel sauce to the blender and gently stir it in with a spoon or rubber spatula. Pour the milkshake into two glasses. Top with whipped cream and maraschino cherries.

TEEN CHEF TIP: The key to delicious milkshakes is only mixing everything long enough to incorporate the ingredients, without pulverizing them or blending too much so that you lose the pieces of filling. Only using high speed initially, and then mixing in low speed can maintain the texture of your milkshake and preserve the tidbits of tasty additions.

ACKNOWLEDGMENTS

Thank you to Sarah and the team at Page Street for the opportunity to write a second cookbook! Thank you for all the insights and push to make this cookbook the best it could be. Once again, you were an absolute pleasure to work with.

Many, many thanks to Ken, whose talent, kindness and dedication takes a collection of recipes and skyrockets them to another level with amazing photography. For the second time, cookbook shooting week was a blur of fun and hard work. I am so thankful to have you on the team!

Thank you to everyone who utilizes my website and trusts me with recipes and tips. My Instagram community's support and feedback over the years has made this job so much fun. Thank you for sharing in my excitement for the vision of this book and hanging out during months of recipe development and writing when there wasn't a lot more I was producing. Y'all are the best, and I hope you love this book.

Thank you to my dear Wild and Free community—both my local friends and all my friends around the country, especially Greta. You are all my people and I am so thankful to be a part of Wild and Free. Thank you for listening to ideas, tasting recipes and offering feedback for months. You make our lives so much richer.

Thank you to Heather, Maria, Kristin and Sara who did all of that and more. This cookbook will forever be tied to memories of our friendship and that makes it all the more special to me. I am deeply thankful for each of you.

To Jack and Jedidiah, my oldest kids and my first kitchen companions. For over a decade, you've been alongside me in the kitchen, learning to cook, keeping me company and enjoying what we make together. Thank you for all the help developing, tasting and testing these recipes. You make your mom very proud, and I hope you feel some ownership over this cookbook too.

To my family as a whole, I know life while writing a cookbook is crazy, and you agreed to do this process another time. Thank you for taking this venture on with me, and for patiently living in the crazy for a season. Molly, Josiah and Marie: You are my little loves and you make me so happy.

Finally, thank you to my best friend and husband, Jeff. I love doing life with you, in and out of the kitchen. Thank you for always believing in me, challenging me to be better and supporting (most) of my crazy ideas. Thank you for helping me with all the time it takes to do this work and for celebrating with me when it was done.

ABOUT THE AUTHOR

Lisa Burns is a self-taught home chef who lives with her husband and five children in North Carolina. A former hater of vegetables and fan of packaged dinners, she now loves growing her own food in her family's garden plot and counts cooking meals from scratch with her kids as one of her favorite things to do. Lisa is passionate about helping families get their children involved in the kitchen too and is now entering the wonderful stage of her kids being old enough (and experienced enough) to start making meals on their own for themselves and the family.

Lisa is the founder of This Pilgrim Life, a website and online community for anyone who enjoys simple, homemade recipes that fit into people's real lives. Her goal is to make whole-food, from-scratch cooking easier and more accessible to everyone. She stays very busy outside of the kitchen with reading, outdoor adventures and creative living.

INDEX

A

Almonds
Hiker's Salad with Creamy Citrus
Poppyseed Dressing, 75
Sweet & Salty White Chocolate
Bark, 125
Amazing Mini Pound Cakes, 152
Apple(s)
Easiest Apple Pie & Homemade
Whipped Cream, 144
Energy-Boosting Green Smoothie,
79
Everyone's Favorite Tuna Salad, 97
Hiker's Salad with Creamy Citrus
Poppyseed Dressing, 75
Sweet & Savory Veggie Soup, 76
Apple butter, in Ridiculously Good
Ham Sliders, 98
Applesauce, in Chocolate Chip Muf-
fins With a Twist, 94
Asparagus, in Perfect Roasted Vege-
tables, 84
Avocado. See also Guacamole
Easy Cheesy Enchiladas, 23
Energy-Boosting Green Smoothie,
79
Peanut Butter & Chocolate Protein
Smoothie, 111
Totally Loaded Nachos, 126
Awesome Black Bean Taquitos, 101
Awesome Caesar Salad Wraps, 72

B

Bacon
Crazy Delicious Hot Dog Bar, 129
Healthy Egg Bites, 115
Overloaded Potato Wedges, 90
Perfect Late-Night Omelet, 66
Baking sheets, 19
Banana Split Milkshakes, 155
Barbecue sauce, in Tater Tot Su-
preme, 39
Batch cooking, 16

Beans
Awesome Black Bean Taquitos, 101
Pasta & Veggie Soup to Fill You
Up, 83
Totally Loaded Nachos, 126
Beef hot dogs, in Crazy Delicious Hot
Dog Bar, 129
Beef, in The Best Steak Ever, 45. See
also Ground beef
Beef stock
Better-For-You Instant Ramen, 89
Epic Meat Lovers' Chili, 54
Pasta & Veggie Soup to Fill You
Up, 83
Bell peppers
Epic Meat Lovers' Chili, 54
Firepit Chicken Fajitas, 134
Unbelievably Delicious Veg Tart,
80
Best Ever Breakfast Sandwiches, 107
The Best Party Popcorn, 133
The Best Steak Ever, 45
Better-Than-Boxed Toaster Pastries,
112
Biscuit dough, in Chicken Pot Pie
Made Easy, 35
Blueberries
dried, in Take-Anywhere Energy
Bites, 102
Super Easy Grab-&-Go Overnight
Oatmeal, 116
Breads and buns. See also Sandwich-
es; Sliders
Cinnamon Raisin Buns, 65
French Bread, 61–62
Hot Dog Bar, 129
Sub Rolls, 61–62
Broccoli florets
Creamy Chicken & Broccoli Soup,
27
Perfect Roasted Vegetables, 84
Brownies, Epic PB Cup, 155
Brown rice, in Creamy Chicken &
Broccoli Soup, 27

Brussels sprouts, in Roasted Sausage
with Perfectly Crisp Potatoes &
Veg, 24
Burgers (Sliders with an Upgrade),
58
Burritos, Killer Breakfast, 119

C

Caesar dressing, in Awesome Caesar
Salad Wraps, 72
Cakes
Amazing Mini Pound Cakes, 152
Last-Minute Confetti Cookie Cake,
148
Legendary Double Cookie Ice
Cream Cake, 143
Campfire, cooking over a, 134
Caramel
The Best Party Popcorn, 133
Legendary Double Cookie Ice
Cream Cake, 143
Super Fun Banana Split Milk-
shakes, 155
Carrots
Chicken Pot Pie Made Easy, 35
Creamy Chicken & Broccoli Soup,
27
Easy Pork Fried Rice, 36
mirepoix mixture with, 35
Perfect Roasted Vegetables, 84
Roasted Sausage with Perfectly
Crisp Potatoes & Veg, 24
Share-The-Love Cozy Chicken
Noodle Soup, 49
Sweet & Savory Veggie Soup, 76
Cast iron pans, 16
Celery
Energy-Boosting Green Smoothie,
79
mirepoix mixture with, 35
Share-The-Love Cozy Chicken
Noodle Soup, 49
Cereal, in Comeback Snack Mix, 138

Cheddar cheese
  Awesome Black Bean Taquitos, 101
  Best Ever Breakfast Sandwiches, 107
  Healthy Egg Bites, 115
  Homestyle Baked Mac 'N' Cheese, 57
  Killer Breakfast Burritos, 119
  Next-Level Grilled Cheese Sandwiches, 93
  Overloaded Potato Wedges, 90
  Totally Loaded Nachos, 126
Cheese. See also Cheddar cheese; Mozzarella cheese; Parmesan cheese
  adding to a sauce, 46
  bagged and pre-shredded, 46
  cotija, in Mexican Street Corn Made Easy, 71
  Easy Cheesy Enchiladas, 23
  Firepit Chicken Fajitas, 134
  Healthy Egg Bites, 115
  Next-Level Grilled Cheese Sandwiches, 93
  Perfect Late-Night Omelet, 66
  Swiss, in Sliders With An Upgrade, 58
  Tater Tot Supreme, 39
  Totally Loaded Nachos, 126
Chef's knife, how to hold, 84
Chia seeds
  Super Easy Grab-&-Go Overnight Oatmeal, 116
  Take-Anywhere Energy Bites, 102
  uses of, 102
Chicken
  Awesome Caesar Salad Wraps, 72
  Chicken Pot Pie Made Easy, 35
  Creamy Chicken & Broccoli Soup, 27
  Firepit Chicken Fajitas, 134
  Share-The-Love Cozy Chicken Noodle Soup, 49
  Sweet & Tangy Grilled Chicken Kabobs, 32
  Your First Amazing Chicken Curry, 31

Chicken stock
  Chicken Pot Pie Made Easy, 35
  Creamy Chicken & Broccoli Soup, 27
  making homemade, 76
  Share-The-Love Cozy Chicken Noodle Soup, 49
  Sweet & Savory Veggie Soup, 76
Chili, Epic Meat Lovers', 54
Chocolate
  The Best Party Popcorn, 133
  melting, 125
  three types used in baking, 155
Chocolate chips and morsels. See also Dark chocolate
  Chocolate Chip Muffins With a Twist, 94
  Epic PB Cup Brownies, 155
  Legendary Double Cookie Ice Cream Cake, 143
  Super Fun Banana Split Milkshakes, 155
  Sweet & Salty White Chocolate Bark, 125
Cilantro
  Easy Cheesy Enchiladas, 23
  Mexican Street Corn Made Easy, 71
Cinnamon Raisin Buns, 65
Citrus fruits/juices
  Chocolate Chip Muffins With a Twist, 94
  Energy-Boosting Green Smoothie, 79
  Hiker's Salad with Creamy Citrus Poppyseed Dressing, 75
  Mexican Street Corn Made Easy, 71
  zesting, 94
Cocoa powder
  about, 155
  Decadent Hot Chocolate with Spruced Up Marshmallows, 137
  Epic PB Cup Brownies, 155
  Homemade Mocha Frappuccino, 120
  Impressive Chocolate Pudding Pie, 151
  Peanut Butter & Chocolate Protein Smoothie, 111

Coconut, in The Best Party Popcorn, 133
Coconut milk, in Your First Amazing Chicken Curry, 31
Coffee, in Homemade Mocha Frappuccino, 120
Coleslaw, Sriracha, 129
Comeback Snack Mix, 138
Cookie Cake, Last-Minute Confetti, 148
Cookie dough
  heat treating flour for, 143
  how long to stir, 148
  Legendary Double Cookie Ice Cream Cake, 143
Cookies
  Legendary Double Cookie Ice Cream Cake, 143
  Ooey-Gooey S'Mores Cookies, 147
Cook, top ten tips for learning how to, 12–19
Corn
  Mexican Street Corn Made Easy, 71
  Tater Tot Supreme, 39
Corn tortillas
  Easy Cheesy Enchiladas, 23
  Firepit Chicken Fajitas, 134
  when to use, 101
Cotija cheese, in Mexican Street Corn Made Easy, 71
Craisins, in Hiker's Salad with Creamy Citrus Poppyseed Dressing, 75
Crazy Delicious Hot Dog Bar, 129
Cream cheese
  Amazing Mini Pound Cakes, 152
  Stuffed French Toast, 108
  Unbelievably Delicious Veg Tart, 80
Creamy Chicken & Broccoli Soup, 27
Croissants, in Best Ever Breakfast Sandwiches, 107
Croutons, in Awesome Caesar Salad Wraps, 72
Cucumber, in Energy-Boosting Green Smoothie, 79
Curry sauce, in Your First Amazing Chicken Curry, 31

D

Dark chocolate
about, 155
Decadent Hot Chocolate with Spruced Up Marshmallows, 137
Impressive Chocolate Pudding Pie, 151
Ooey-Gooey S'Mores Cookies, 147
Decadent Hot Chocolate with Spruced Up Marshmallows, 137
Deli ham, in Ridiculously Good Ham Sliders, 98
Dip, Homemade Potato Chip, 130
Dressings. See also Ranch dressing
Caesar, in Awesome Caesar Salad Wraps, 72
for Hiker's Salad with Creamy Citrus Poppyseed Dressing, 75
making homemade salad, 75
for Roasted Sausage with Perfectly Crisp Potatoes & Veg, 24
Dried fruit, in Take-Anywhere Energy Bites, 102

E

Easiest Apple Pie & Homemade Whipped Cream, 144
Easy Cheesy Enchiladas, 23
Easy Pork Fried Rice, 36
Egg(s)
Best Ever Breakfast Sandwiches, 107
Healthy Egg Bites, 115
Killer Breakfast Burritos, 119
making fluffy scrambled, 119
Perfect Late-Night Omelet, 66
Stuffed French Toast, 108
Enchiladas, Easy Cheesy, 23
Energy Bites, Take-Anywhere, 102
Energy-Boosting Green Smoothie, 79
Epic Meat Lovers' Chili, 54
Epic PB Cup Brownies, 155
Equipment. See Kitchen tools and equipment
Everyone's Favorite Tuna Salad, 97

F

Fajitas, Firepit Chicken, 134
Fancy Lasagna With No Layering, 40
Feta cheese, in Healthy Egg Bites, 115
Firepit Chicken Fajitas, 134
Flour, heat-treating, 143
Flour tortillas
Awesome Black Bean Taquitos, 101
Awesome Caesar Salad Wraps, 72
Killer Breakfast Burritos, 119
Frappuccino, Homemade Mocha, 120
Freezing food
green smoothie packets, 79
leftovers, 16
mirepoix mixture, 35
rice, 31
French Bread, 61–62
French Toast, Stuffed, 108
Fried Rice, Easy Pork, 36
Frittatas, mini, 115
Frozen vegetables, Pasta & Veggie Soup to Fill You Up, 83. See also Corn; Peas

G

Glazes
for Better-Than-Boxed Toaster Pastries, 112
for Cinnamon Raisin Buns, 65
Graham crackers
Impressive Chocolate Pudding Pie, 151
Ooey-Gooey S'Mores Cookies, 147
Grease, draining from a pan, 39
Greek yogurt
Awesome Black Bean Taquitos, 101
Homemade Potato Chip Dip, 130
Mexican Street Corn Made Easy, 71
Peanut Butter & Chocolate Protein Smoothie, 111
as a substitute for sour cream, 126
Super Easy Grab-&-Go Overnight Oatmeal, 116
Totally Loaded Nachos, 126

Your First Amazing Chicken Curry, 31
Green chiles, in Awesome Black Bean Taquitos, 101
Green onions
Better-For-You Instant Ramen, 89
growing your own, 80
Mexican Street Corn Made Easy, 71
Overloaded Potato Wedges, 90
Tater Tot Supreme, 39
Unbelievably Delicious Veg Tart, 80
Green peppers
Easy Cheesy Enchiladas, 23
Homemade Meatball Sub Sandwiches, 28
Killer Breakfast Burritos, 119
Green Smoothie, Energy-Boosting, 79
Grilled-Cheese Sandwiches, 93
Ground beef
Easy Cheesy Enchiladas, 23
Epic Meat Lovers' Chili, 54
Fancy Lasagna With No Layering, 40
Now & Later Spaghetti Bake, 53
Sliders with an Upgrade, 58
Ground sausage, in Tater Tot Supreme, 39
Gruyere cheese, in Next-Level Grilled Cheese Sandwiches, 93
Guacamole
Awesome Black Bean Taquitos, 101
Crazy Delicious Hot Dog Bar, 129
Easy Cheesy Enchiladas, 23
Firepit Chicken Fajitas, 134
Totally Loaded Nachos, 126

H

Half and half, in Decadent Hot Chocolate with Spruced Up Marshmallows, 137
Ham (deli), in Ridiculously Good Ham Sliders, 98
Healthy Egg Bites, 115

Heat-treating flour, 143
Heavy cream
   The Best Party Popcorn, 133
   Creamy Chicken & Broccoli Soup, 27
   Easiest Apple Pie & Homemade Whipped Cream, 144
   Healthy Egg Bites, 115
   Homemade Mocha Frappuccino, 120
   Impressive Chocolate Pudding Pie, 151
Hiker's Salad with Creamy Citrus Poppyseed Dressing, 75
Homemade Bread in 1 Hour, 61–65
Homemade Meatball Sub Sandwiches, 28
Homemade Mocha Frappuccino, 120
Homemade Potato Chip Dip, 130
Homemade stock, 49
Homestyle Baked Mac 'N' Cheese, 57
Honey
   Chocolate Chip Muffins With a Twist, 94
   Honey Yogurt Drizzle, 76
   Peanut Butter & Chocolate Protein Smoothie, 111
   Sweet & Tangy Grilled Chicken Kabobs, 32
   Take-Anywhere Energy Bites, 102
Hot Chocolate with Spruced Up Marshmallows, 137
Hot Dog Bar, Crazy Delicious, 129

I
Ice cream
   Legendary Double Cookie Ice Cream Cake, 143
   Super Fun Banana Split Milkshakes, 155
Immersion blender, 76
Impressive Chocolate Pudding Pie, 151
Ingredients, prepping, 15

J
Jalapeños
   Crazy Delicious Hot Dog Bar, 129
   Easy Cheesy Enchiladas, 23
   Totally Loaded Nachos, 126
Jam
   Better-Than-Boxed Toaster Pastries, 112
   making homemade, 108
   Stuffed French Toast, 108

K
Kabobs, Sweet & Tangy Grilled Chicken, 32
Killer Breakfast Burritos, 119
Killer Fettuccine Alfredo, 46
Kitchen tools and equipment
   baking sheets, 19
   cast-iron pans, 16
   chef's knife, holding a, 84
   focus on quality vs. quantity for, 12
   immersion blender, 76
   microplane, 94
   for one-pan meals, 21
Knives, 12, 84

L
Lasagna With No Layering, Fancy, 40
Last-Minute Confetti Cookie Cake, 148
Leftovers
   freezing, 16
   reheating pasta, 57
   rice, 36
   soup with pasta or rice, 83
Legendary Double Cookie Ice Cream Cake, 143
Lettuces
   Awesome Caesar Salad Wraps, 72
   Firepit Chicken Fajitas, 134

M
Mac 'N' Cheese, Homestyle Baked, 57
Maillard reaction, 16
Maple syrup
   Easiest Apple Pie & Homemade Whipped Cream, 144
   Homemade Mocha Frappuccino, 120
Maraschino cherries, in Super Fun Banana Split Milkshakes, 155
Marinara sauce
   Fancy Lasagna With No Layering, 40
   Homemade Meatball Sub Sandwiches, 28
   making homemade, 40
   Now & Later Spaghetti Bake, 53
Marshmallows
   Decadent Hot Chocolate with Spruced Up Marshmallows, 137
   Ooey-Gooey S'Mores Cookies, 147
Mayonnaise
   Everyone's Favorite Tuna Salad, 97
   Hiker's Salad with Creamy Citrus Poppyseed Dressing, 75
   homemade, 97
   Homemade Potato Chip Dip, 130
   Mexican Street Corn Made Easy, 71
   Sriracha Coleslaw, 129
Meatball Sub Sandwiches, 28
Mexican blend cheese
   Easy Cheesy Enchiladas, 23
   Totally Loaded Nachos, 126
Mexican Street Corn Made Easy
   Crazy Delicious Hot Dog Bar, 129
   recipe, 71
Microplanes, 94
Microwave, using a damp paper towel in the, 90
Milkshakes, Super Fun Banana Split, 156
Mirepoix, 35

Mozzarella cheese
   Fancy Lasagna With No Layering, 40
   Homemade Meatball Sub Sandwiches, 28
   Now & Later Spaghetti Bake, 53
   Ridiculously Good Ham Sliders, 98
   Super Easy Pizza with Endless Possibilities, 50
Muffins, Chocolate Chip, 94
Mushrooms, in Sliders with an Upgrade, 59

N

Naan bread, with Your First Amazing Chicken Curry, 31
Nachos, Totally Loaded, 126
Next-Level Grilled Cheese Sandwiches, 93
Now & Later Spaghetti Bake, 53
Nuts
   Comeback Snack Mix, 138
   Hiker's Salad with Creamy Citrus Poppyseed Dressing, 75
   Super Fun Banana Split Milkshakes, 156
   Sweet & Salty White Chocolate Bark, 125
   Your First Amazing Chicken Curry, 31

O

Oats
   Chocolate Chip Muffins With a Twist, 94
   Super Easy Grab-&-Go Overnight Oatmeal, 116
   Take-Anywhere Energy Bites, 102
   types of, 116
Omelet, Perfect Late-Night, 66
Onion(s). See also Yellow onions
   Chicken Pot Pie Made Easy, 35
   Killer Breakfast Burritos, 119
   mirepoix mixture using, 35
   Share-The-Love Cozy Chicken Noodle Soup, 49
Ooey-Gooey S'Mores Cookies, 147

Orange juice/zest
   Chocolate Chip Muffins With a Twist, 94
   Energy-Boosting Green Smoothie, 79
Overloaded Potato Wedges, 90
Overnight Oatmeal, Super Easy Grab-&-Go, 116

P

Pans
   draining grease from, 39
   for sautéing, 16
Parmesan cheese
   Creamy Chicken & Broccoli Soup, 27
   Fancy Lasagna With No Layering, 40
   Killer Fettuccine Alfredo, 46
   Now & Later Spaghetti Bake, 53
   Pasta & Veggie Soup to Fill You Up, 83
   Perfect Roasted Vegetables, 84
   Share-The-Love Cozy Chicken Noodle Soup, 49
   Unbelievably Delicious Veg Tart, 80
Pasta
   Fancy Lasagna With No Layering, 40
   five principles to know for cooking, 53
   Homestyle Baked Mac 'N' Cheese, 57
   Killer Fettuccine Alfredo, 46
   Now & Later Spaghetti Bake, 53
   Pasta & Veggie Soup to Fill You Up, 83
   reheating dishes of, 57
   Share-The-Love Cozy Chicken Noodle Soup, 49
Pastries, Better-Than-Boxed Toaster, 112
Peanut butter
   Epic PB Cup Brownies, 155
   Peanut Butter & Chocolate Protein Smoothie, 111
   Take-Anywhere Energy Bites, 102
Peanut Butter & Chocolate Protein Smoothie, 111

Peas
   Chicken Pot Pie Made Easy, 35
   Easy Pork Fried Rice, 36
   Your First Amazing Chicken Curry, 31
Peppermint, in Decadent Hot Chocolate with Spruced Up Marshmallows, 137
Perfect Late-Night Omelet, 66
Perfect Roasted Vegetables, 84
Pesto sauce
   making your own, 93
   Next-Level Grilled Cheese Sandwiches, 93
Pickled red onions
   Crazy Delicious Hot Dog Bar, 129
   Totally Loaded Nachos, 126
Pickle juice, in Comeback Snack Mix, 138
Pickles, in Everyone's Favorite Tuna Salad, 97
Pico De Gallo, Easy Cheesy Enchilada with, 2323
Pies and pie dough
   Better-Than-Boxed Toaster Pastries, 112
   Easiest Apple Pie & Homemade Whipped Cream, 144
   Impressive Chocolate Pudding Pie, 151
Pimento cheese, in Crazy Delicious Hot Dog Bar, 129
Pizza, Super Easy with Endless Possibilities, 50
Popcorn, The Best Party, 133
Poppyseed Dressing, Hiker's Salad with Creamy Citrus, 75
Pork. See also Bacon
   Easy Pork Fried Rice, 36
   Ridiculously Good Ham Sliders, 98
Potato Chip Dip, 130
Potato chips, in Sweet & Salty White Chocolate Bark, 125
Potatoes
   Overloaded Potato Wedges, 90
   Roasted Sausage with Perfectly Crisp Potatoes & Veg, 24
Pound Cakes, Amazing Mini, 152
Prepping ingredients, 15

Pretzels
  Comeback Snack Mix, 138
  Sweet & Salty White Chocolate
    Bark, 125
Pudding Pie, Impressive Chocolate,
  151
Puff pastry, in Unbelievably Delicious
  Veg Tart, 80

Q

Quality ingredients, importance of, 15

R

Raisins
  Cinnamon Raisin Buns, 65
  Everyone's Favorite Tuna Salad, 97
  Take-Anywhere Energy Bites, 102
Ramen, Better-For-You Instant, 89
Ranch dressing
  homemade, 90
  Overloaded Potato Wedges, 90
  Tater Tot Supreme, 39
Recipes
  reading the entire, 15
  trying new variations of, 15
Red onion, in Your First Amazing
  Curry, 31. See also Pickled red
  onions
Ribeye steam
  The Best Steak Ever, 45
  Salad Wrap using leftover, 72
Rice
  chilling for fried rice, 36
  Creamy Chicken & Broccoli Soup,
    27
  Easy Pork Fried Rice, 36
  freezing and reheating, 31
  Your First Amazing Chicken Curry,
    31
Ricotta cheese, in Fancy Lasagna
  With No Layering, 40
Ridiculously Good Ham Sliders, 98
Roasted Sausage with Perfectly Crisp
  Potatoes & Veg, 24
Roasting foods, 19, 24
Rolls, Sub, 62
Romaine lettuce, in Awesome Caesar
  Salad Wraps, 72
Rotisserie chicken, in Chicken Pot Pie
  Made Easy, 35

S

Safety precautions
  eating raw cookie dough, 143
  holding a chef's knife, 84
  when slicing jalapeños, 23
Salad dressings. See Dressings
Salad greens, in Hiker's Salad with
  Creamy Citrus Poppyseed Dress-
  ing, 75
Salad Wraps, 72
Salad wraps, Awesome Caesar, 72
Salmon, in Salad Wrap, 72
Salsa
  Awesome Black Bean Taquitos, 101
  Easy Cheesy Enchiladas, 23
  Firepit Chicken Fajitas, 134
  Killer Breakfast Burritos, 119
  Totally Loaded Nachos, 126
Sandwiches. See also Sliders
  Best Ever Breakfast Sandwiches,
    107
  Homemade Meatball Sub Sand-
    wiches, 28
  Next-Level Grilled Cheese Sand-
    wiches, 93
  Stuffed French Toast, 108
Sausage
  Best Ever Breakfast Sandwiches,
    107
  Roasted Sausage with Perfectly
    Crisp Potatoes & Veg, 24
  Tater Tot Supreme, 39
Sautéing, 16
Scrambled eggs, in Killer Breakfast
  Burritos, 119
Semi-sweet chocolate
  about, 155
  Epic PB Cup Brownies, 155
Simple syrup, 137
Sliders
  Ridiculously Good Ham Sliders, 98
  Sliders with an Upgrade, 58
Smoothies
  Energy-Boosting Green Smoothie,
    79
  Peanut Butter & Chocolate Protein
    Smoothie, 111
Snack Mix, 138

Soups
  Creamy Chicken & Broccoli Soup,
    27
  homemade stock for, 49
  as leftovers, 83
  Pasta & Veggie Soup to Fill You
    Up, 83
  Share-The-Love Cozy Chicken
    Noodle Soup, 49
  Sweet & Savory Veggie Soup, 76
Sour cream
  Awesome Black Bean Taquitos, 101
  Easy Cheesy Enchiladas, 23
  Epic Meat Lovers' Chili, 54
  Firepit Chicken Fajitas, 134
  Greek yogurt used as a substitute
    for, 126
  Tater Tot Supreme, 39
Spaghetti Bake, 53
Spinach
  Energy-Boosting Green Smoothie,
    79
  Fancy Lasagna With No Layering,
    40
  Healthy Egg Bites, 115
Sprinkles
  Decadent Hot Chocolate with
    Spruced Up Marshmallows, 137
  Last-Minute Confetti Cookie Cake,
    148
Squash, in Sweet & Tangy Grilled
  Chicken Kabobs, 32
Sriracha Coleslaw, 129
Steak
  The Best Steak Ever, 45
  leftover, in Salad Wrap, 72
Stew meat, in Epic Meat Lovers' Chili,
  54
Stuffed French Toast, 108
Sub rolls
  Homemade Meatball Sub Sand-
    wiches, 28
  recipe, 61–62
Sugar glaze, 112
Sunflower seeds
  Hiker's Salad with Creamy Citrus
    Poppyseed Dressing, 75
  Take-Anywhere Energy Bites, 102
Super Easy Grab-&-Go Overnight
  Oatmeal, 116

Super Fun Banana Split Milkshakes, 155, 156
Sweet & Salty White Chocolate Bark, 125
Sweet & Savory Veggie Soup, 76
Sweet & Tangy Grilled Chicken Kabobs, 32
Swiss cheese, in Sliders with an Upgrade, 59

T

Take-Anywhere Energy Bites, 102
Taquitos, Awesome Black Bean, 101
Tater tots, in Tater Tot Supreme, 39
Tomatoes
    Easy Cheesy Enchiladas, 23
    Epic Meat Lovers' Chili, 54
    Firepit Chicken Fajitas, 134
    Salad Wraps, 72
    Unbelievably Delicious Veg Tart, 80
Tomato paste/sauce, in Pasta & Veggie Soup to Fill You Up, 83
Tools, kitchen. See Kitchen tools and equipment
Tortilla chips
    Awesome Black Bean Taquitos, 101
    Easy Cheesy Enchiladas, 23
    Totally Loaded Nachos, 126
Totally Loaded Nachos, 126
Tuna
    Everyone's Favorite Tuna Salad, 97
    Salad Wrap, 72

V

Vacuum sealers, 138
Vegetables, sautéing, 16. See also specific vegetables

W

Whipped cream
    Easiest Apple Pie & Homemade Whipped Cream, 144
    Homemade Mocha Frappuccino, 120
    Impressive Chocolate Pudding Pie, 151
    Legendary Double Cookie Ice Cream Cake, 143
    making homemade, 120
    Super Fun Banana Split Milkshakes, 155
Wild rice, in Creamy Chicken & Broccoli Soup, 27
Worcestershire sauce
    homemade barbecue sauce, 39
    Pasta & Veggie Soup to Fill You Up, 83
    Sliders with an Upgrade, 58
Wraps, Awesome Caesar Salad, 72

Y

Yellow onions
    Creamy Chicken & Broccoli Soup, 27
    Easy Cheesy Enchiladas, 23
    Easy Pork Fried Rice, 36
    Epic Meat Lovers' Chili, 54
    Firepit Chicken Fajitas, 134
    Homemade Meatball Sub Sandwiches, 28
    Pasta & Veggie Soup to Fill You Up, 83
    Roasted Sausage with Perfectly Crisp Potatoes & Veg, 24
    Sweet & Savory Veggie Soup, 76
    Your First Amazing Chicken Curry, 31
Yellow squash, in Sweet & Tangy Grilled Chicken Kabobs, 32
Yogurt Drizzle, for Sweet & Savory Veggie Soup, 76
Your First Amazing Chicken Curry, 31

Z

Zest, citrus fruit, 94
Zipper storage bags, vacuum sealing, 138
Zucchini, in Sweet & Tangy Grilled Chicken Kabobs, 32